hamlyn
QuickCook

hamlyn

QuickCook
Cakes and Bakes

Recipes by Jo McAuley

Every dish, three ways – you choose!
30 minutes | 20 minutes | 10 minutes

An Hachette UK Company
www.hachette.co.uk

First published in Great Britain in 2012 by Hamlyn,
a division of Octopus Publishing Group Ltd
Endeavour House, 189 Shaftesbury Avenue
London WC2H 8JY
www.octopusbooks.co.uk

Copyright © Octopus Publishing Group Ltd 2012

ISBN 978-0-600-62491-2

A CIP catalogue record for this book is available from the British Library

Printed and bound in China

10 9 8 7 6 5 4 3 2 1

Both metric and imperial measurements are given for the recipes. Use one set of
measures only, not a mixture of both.

Standard level spoon measurements are used in all recipes
1 tablespoon = 15 ml
1 teaspoon = 5 ml

Ovens should be preheated to the specified temperature. If using a fan-assisted oven,
follow the manufacturer's instructions for adjusting the time and temperature. Grills
should also be preheated.

This book includes dishes made with nuts and nut derivatives. It is advisable for
those with known allergic reactions to nuts and nut derivatives and those who may
be potentially vulnerable to these allergies, such as pregnant and nursing mothers,
invalids, the elderly, babies and children, to avoid dishes made with nuts and nut oils.

It is also prudent to check the labels of preprepared ingredients for the possible
inclusion of nut derivatives.

The Department of Health advises that eggs should not be consumed raw. This book
contains some dishes made with raw or lightly cooked eggs. It is prudent for more
vulnerable people such as pregnant and nursing mothers, invalids, the elderly, babies
and young children to avoid uncooked or lightly cooked dishes made with eggs.

Contents

Introduction

30 20 10 – Quick, Quicker, Quickest

This book offers a new and flexible approach to meal-planning for busy cooks and lets you choose the recipe option that best fits the time you have available. Inside you will find 360 dishes that will inspire you and motivate you to get cooking every day of the year. All the recipes take a maximum of 30 minutes to cook. Some take as little as 20 minutes and, amazingly, many take only 10 minutes. With a bit of preparation, you can easily try out one new recipe from this book each night and slowly you will build a wide and exciting portfolio of recipes to suit your needs.

How Does it Work?

Every recipe in the QuickCook series can be cooked one of three ways – a 30-minute version, a 20-minute version or a super-quick and easy 10-minute version. At the beginning of each chapter you'll find recipes listed by time. Choose a dish based on how much time you have and turn to that page.

You'll find the main recipe in the middle of the page with a beautiful photograph and two time-variations below.

If you enjoy the dish, you can go back and cook the other time options. If you liked the 30-minute Caramel Chocolate Fondants (see pages 74–75), but only have 10 minutes to spare, then you'll find a way to cook them using cheat ingredients or clever shortcuts.

If you love the flavours of the 10-minute Tomato and Olive Filo Tartlets (see pages 250–251), why not try something more substantial such as the 20-minute Tomato and Olive Tarts, or be inspired to cook a more elaborate meal using similar ingredients, such as the 30-minute Tomato and Olive Tarte Tatin. Alternatively, browse through all of the 360 delicious recipes, find something that catches your eye and then cook the version that fits your time frame.

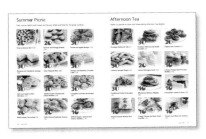

Or, for easy inspiration, turn to the gallery on pages 12–19 to get an instant overview by themes, such as Summer Picnic or Afternoon Tea.

QuickCook online

To make life even easier, you can use the special code on each recipe page to email yourself a recipe card for printing, or email a text-only shopping list to your phone. Go to www.hamlynquickcook.com and enter the recipe code at the bottom of each page.

 CAK-PIES-CUP

QuickCook Cakes and Bakes

What could be lovelier than the smell of muffins still warm from the oven, home-baked in ess than 30 minutes? In the time it would take to get to the supermarket and back with an industrially produced, unsatisfying snack high in sugar and fat, you could already be savouring your own, delicious produce. Whether you are an established cook or a novice baker, there are lots of recipes in this book that will appeal with a time-frame to suit you. So let's get baking!

Equipment

When baking, your oven is the most essential piece of equipment, so check that it is working properly and stays at a reliable temperature. If you are at all unsure, invest in an oven thermometer to verify your oven's accuracy. The temperatures in this book are given for a standard oven. If you are cooking with a fan oven you will need to decrease the temperature by 20°C (50°F) or alternatively, just reduce the cooking time slightly, checking for 'doneness' to see if it's ready. Refer to the manufacturer's instructions for more details. A fan oven ensures an even temperature throughout the oven, which means that you don't need to change tray position during cooking and your cakes and cookies will be evenly baked. When using a standard oven, be sure to space your shelves evenly and for anything not likely to sink, swap the trays around midway through cooking.

Another important piece of equipment is a timer, preferably with both minutes and seconds. If your oven does not have one, get a basic, battery-operated timer.

A reliable set of weighing scales is essential — correct measuring equipment will help you achieve perfect results. Electronic scales are preferable for accuracy and ease, but whichever type you are most comfortable using is fine. You can also buy a set of proper measuring spoons very cheaply.

To enjoy your baked delights at their best, it is important to cool items on wire cooling racks when instructed to do so in the recipe. They allow the air to circulate, which will avoid soggy-bottomed cookies and scones.

Try to use baking tins with dimensions as close as possible to those recommended in the recipes, as altering the size of a tin too much may lead to poor results. A set of solid baking tins seems like quite an investment, but may save money in the long run. Usually thinner and of poor quality, cheap tins can rust, warp and lose their shape over time. Buy your cake tins from a reputable dealer, or check out second-hand sales for good quality tins for less money. Silicone bakeware is also available, and is popular due to its non-stick properties. Do some research, and choose tins that will suit you.

It is important to line your tins and trays properly, according to the use they are being put to. For tray-baked goods such as cookies, scones and rockcakes, it is highly recommended to line the trays first. You can use baking parchment, but why not invest in a couple of reusable, heat-resistant, nonstick liners? They can be cut to the perfect size to line your tins, and are also useful as a surface for rolling out pastries and doughs.

When lining tins for brownies and traybakes, cut a length of baking parchment that is the same width as your tin but a few centimetres longer, so that it overlaps at the ends. This way you can just run a round-bladed knife along the lengths, and carefully lift out the whole cake to transfer to a cooling rack.

You have a range of different options when making individual small bakes such as muffins and cupcakes. Use standard-sized muffin moulds lined with paper cases for cupcakes, and make muffins in case-lined or greased, nonstick muffin moulds. You can vary the size by using giant or mini muffin moulds, making sure to adjust the cooking time accordingly. You can also buy tins with different shaped moulds, such as mini loaves.

Some other equipment mentioned in this book:
· A range of plain and fluted cookie cutters, which can also be used when making scones.
· An electric hand whisk or stand-alone whisk, which will save time and effort and lead to lighter, airier results.
· Mini choppers and food processors will make light work of laborious, time-consuming tasks such as chopping nuts, chocolate and other ingredients.

• A rubber spatula is extremely useful for scraping and stirring, especially for making brownies when you do not want to incorporate too much air into the batter.
• A palette knife for spreading and lifting.
• A plastic or metal mesh sieve for sifting flour and icing sugar – essential if you want to avoid heavy, lumpy cake mixtures.
• A range of bowls in different sizes will make weighing and mixing ingredients much easier.
• Piping bags and nozzles, for decorating cupcakes and cookies. You can buy rolls of throw-away piping bags, which cuts down on the washing up and allows you to have different colours of icings on the go at the same time. If you will be doing a lot of cake decorating, invest in washable piping bags.

Ingredients

Always use the best-quality ingredients available to you and your budget, as they will affect the final taste and appearance of your baking. Measure ingredients carefully and follow the instructions in the method and the order in which they are added. Some ingredients are easily interchangeable, such as substituting walnuts for pecans, but the standard recipe should remain unaltered: that is to say, always use the correct type of flour, the stated quantity of raising agent, and the right number and size of eggs. Unless instructed otherwise, use ingredients at room temperature – this can have a big impact on how your cakes rise and your cookies crumble. Try to use free-range eggs whenever possible; your guilt-free, home-baked goodies will taste better than ever. Butter should be unsalted, unless stated otherwise.

Chocolate does not need to be the most expensive variety in the shop, but it does need to be suitable for baking. Dark chocolate with a minimum 70% cocoa-solid content is recommended. You can buy dark, milk and white chocolate chunks and chips for baking which are the perfect size for adding to your recipes and cut down on preparation time. Whenever possible, melt your chocolate in a 'double boiler' or a bowl placed over a pan of barely simmering water, making sure that the bowl doesn't touch the surface of the water. It is also possible to melt chocolate in the microwave. Use low power and check frequently to make sure that it doesn't burn.

There are many exciting flavourings that you can add to pretty much any recipe. For simple added flavour, try incorporating finely grated orange, lemon or lime rind to your baking. You can also experiment with anything from vanilla bean paste to coconut or peppermint extract, available from most big supermarkets or specialist food or bakeware shops. Using pure extracts rather than essences will make for better taste.

A few tips for perfect bakes

There are all sorts of different cookie recipes in this book, something for every occasion. Store chewy-textured cookies in an air-tight container and crunchy cookies in a corked cookie jar, which allows a small amount of air to circulate. This will help to keep them crisp. If you are making several types of cookies with different flavours, make sure you store them separately in the appropriate style of container to avoid ruining their flavours.

Freshly baked scones should be risen, golden and light-textured. To achieve perfect scones, don't overwork the dough. When cutting them out, use a sharp cutter and make sure you don't twist it as you stamp out rounds. Scones are definitely best eaten the day they are baked. If you want to eat them the next day, pop them into the oven for a couple of minutes to freshen them up.

Muffins have a very specific texture, which is achieved with minimal effort and minimal mixing. It is essential not to over-mix a muffin batter to avoid ending up with heavy, unappealing muffins. Use a spring-loaded ice-cream scoop to fill your moulds with less mess.

When making brownies, whisk the sugar with the eggs before adding the remaining ingredients, to encourage the traditional thin, crisp topping. Remove brownies from the oven before they seem quite ready, as they will continue to firm up as they cool. If overcooked, they will become drier and more cake-like. Don't overbeat the brownie batter – you are not trying to encourage air into the mixture, unlike most other cake recipes.

Great for Kids

Tempt young chefs into the kitchen with the occasional sweet indulgence

Peanut Butter Sandwich Cookies 28

Gingerbread Men 30

Banoffee Chip Bites 42

Chopped Nut Snickerdoodles 44

Giant C'raisin Cookies 48

Banana and Caramel Sponge Tart 94

Sticky Pecan Pie 104

Mint and Chocolate Fudge Brownie Sundaes 174

Rocky Road Brownie Bites 180

Banana and Walnut Fudge Brownies 204

Toffee Apple Mini Traybakes 208

Cookie Dough Brownies 226

Party Time

Make your guests feel special by offering them home-baked treats

Nutty Florentine Bites 58

Pear Samosas with Ginger Sauce 86

Chocolate Orange Madeleines 150

Lime and Coconut Snowballs 152

Blackcurrant Swirl Blondies 196

Pecan Cream Brownie Bites 210

Pizza Palmiers 236

Red Pepper and Goats' Cheese Quiches 244

Mini Sausage, Sage and Onion Rolls 248

Smoked Salmon and Chive Pinwheels 254

Cheese and Chive Crisps 258

Spicy Dippers 264

Summer Picnic

Pack a picnic basket with sweet and savoury treats and head for the great outdoors

Cherry Almond Tart 100

Apricot and Orange Friands 140

Prune and Apple Wedges 176

Blackcurrant Sandwich Sponge 188

Oaty Flapjack Slice 200

Orange and Hazelnut Crumble Cake 224

Herb and Seed Scottish Oatcakes 232

Seeded Goats' Cheese and Chive Muffins 238

Courgette and Feta Rockcakes 240

Black Pepper Savouries 246

Chilli Cheese Explosion Scones 260

Grilled Pepper, Spinach and Cheese Muffins 278

Afternoon Tea

Make it a special occasion with these dainty Afternoon Tea delights

Orangey Petticoat Tails 32

Powdery Almond and Vanilla Crackles 34

Cappuccino Cookies 52

Lemony Sponge Fingers 66

Lemon Meringue Fools 108

Lemony Poppy Seed Frosted Muffins 134

Traditional Fruity Rockcakes 182

Wholemeal Sultana Pikelets 192

Devonshire Cream Scones 206

Maple Frosted Walnut Slice 218

Cream Cheese and Herb Toast Soufflés 242

Tomato and Olive Filo Tartlets 250

Pretty & Pink

Sweet treats taste even better if they look good – and few things are prettier than pink

Cherry Coconut Drops 36

Sweetie Jar Moments 62

Strawberry Ricotta Tartlets 72

Cherry Cream Horns 76

Fruit and Marzipan Cobbler 110

Victoria Sponge Cupcakes 122

Turkish Delight Cakes with Rosewater Cream 126

Honeyed Cherry Friands 132

Shimmery Cupcakes 158

White Chocolate and Raspberry Trifle Slices 168

Swiss Roll Baked Alaskas 184

Quick Coconut Lamingtons 220

Very Berry

Few can resist the jewel-like colours and mouth-watering flavours that berries bring

Jammy Jewelled Bites 24

Vanilla and Berry-Soaked Sponge Puddings 78

Cookie Dough Fruit Crumbles 82

White Chocolate and Raspberry Baskets 88

Fruity Gratin Sponge Gratin 92

Crunchy Peach and Strawberry Cranachan 96

Blackberry Fools with Almond Tuiles 98

Blueberry and Mandarin Puffs 116

Blueberry and Vanilla Iced Cupcakes 130

White Chocolate and Raspberry Bran Muffins 138

Chocolate Berry Roulade 172

Blueberry, Cinnamon and Honey Welsh Cakes 212

For Chocolate Lovers

A sumptuous selection for the most discerning chocoholics

Digestive-Coated Ice Cream 40

Chocolate Viennese Whirls 46

Really Chocolatey Choc Chunk Cookies 54

White Chocolate and Macadamia Cookies 64

Caramel Chocolate Fondants 74

Pistachio and Chocolate Danish Pastries 80

Crunchy Chocolate Pears 106

Peanut Butter and Chocolate Mini Muffins 148

Cookies and Cream Whoopie Pies 154

Triple Chocolate Fudge Cupcakes 156

Double Fruit and Nut Brownies 190

Banana and Chocolate Pancakes 222

Decadent Treats

When you are in the mood for pure indulgence, switch off the phone and enjoy ...

Clove and Cardamom Spice Cookies 56

Caramelized Pear Tarte Tatin 84

Amaretti Affogato 112

Peachy Yogurt Brûlée 114

Upside-Down Pineapple and Apricot Muffins 128

Spiced Ginger Cupcakes 136

Maple and Macadamia Madeleines 146

Drop Scones with Ginger Syrup 186

Chocolate Sponge Puddings with Praline Sauce 194

Meringue Blondies with Boozy Cherries 214

Chicken and Taleggio Deep-Filled Pies 262

Blue Cheese and Parma Ham Cigars 270

QuickCook
Biscuits

Recipes listed by cooking time

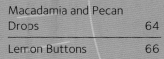

Jammy Jewelled Bites

Makes 22–24

175 g (6 oz) unsalted butter, softened
150 g (5 oz) golden caster sugar
1 large egg, lightly beaten
75 g (3 oz) ground almonds
250 g (8 oz) plain flour
about 4 tablespoons good-quality jam, such as raspberry, apricot or blackcurrant
icing sugar, for dusting

- Line 2 large baking sheets with nonstick baking paper. Place the butter and sugar in a bowl and beat together with a hand-held electric whisk until light and fluffy. Add the egg and ground almonds and beat well. Add the flour and mix to form a soft dough.

- Roll the dough into 22–24 walnut-sized balls, then place on the prepared baking sheets and flatten gently. Use your fingertip or a wooden spoon handle to create dips in the dough. Fill each one with ½ teaspoon of the jam, using a mixture of flavours, if liked.

- Bake in a preheated oven, 200°C (400°F), Gas Mark 6, for 12 minutes, or until lightly golden. Leave to cool slightly on the sheets, then transfer to wire racks to cool completely. Serve dusted with icing sugar.

Jammy Buttercream Bites

Place 50 g (2 oz) softened unsalted butter and 75 g (3 oz) sifted icing sugar in a small bowl and beat together with a hand-held electric whisk until smooth. Spread the buttercream over 12 plain cookies and top each one with ½ teaspoon jam. Top each with a second biscuit and sandwich together. Serve dusted with icing sugar.

Jammy Dodgers

Place 150 g (5 oz) softened unsalted butter, 125 g (4 oz) golden caster sugar and 1 teaspoon vanilla bean paste or extract in a bowl and beat together with a hand-held electric whisk until light and fluffy. Beat in 2 large egg yolks, then add 250 g (8 oz) plain flour and mix to form a soft but not sticky dough. Roll out on a floured surface to 2–3 mm (⅛ inch) thick, then stamp out 15–20 rounds from half the dough using a 6 cm (2½ inch) plain cutter; stamp out 15–20 rounds from the remaining dough using a 6 cm (2½ inch) fluted cutter. Cut out a small circle or shape from the centre of the fluted rounds. Place on 2 large baking sheets lined with nonstick baking paper and bake in a preheated oven, 200°C (400°F), Gas Mark 6, for 10–12 minutes, or until pale golden. Leave to cool on the sheets for 1 minute, then transfer to wire racks to cool completely. Once cool, spread about 4 tablespoons jam between the plain cookies, then top with the fluted cookies and sandwich together. Serve dusted with icing sugar.

Fudge and Oat Cookies

Makes 18–20

100 g (3½ oz) unsalted butter
1 tablespoon honey or agave
  syrup
100 g (3½ oz) rolled oats
1 teaspoon vanilla extract
1 teaspoon bicarbonate of soda
125 g (4 oz) plain flour
125 g (4 oz) soft light brown sugar
50 g (2 oz) mini fudge chunks

- Line 2 baking sheets with nonstick baking paper. Place the butter, honey or agave syrup, oats, vanilla extract and bicarbonate of soda in a saucepan over a low heat and warm gently until the butter has melted. Stir well, then leave to cool for 5 minutes.

- Scrape the mixture into a large bowl and stir in the flour and sugar. Add the fudge chunks and mix until combined. Roll the mixture into 18–20 balls, then place on the prepared baking sheets and flatten gently.

- Bake in a preheated oven, 200°C (400°F), Gas Mark 6, for 10–12 minutes until deep golden. Leave to cool on the sheets for 1 minute, then transfer to wire racks to cool and harden.

 ### Fudge and Oat Cookie Sundaes

Place 150 g (5 oz) vanilla fudge, 150 ml (¼ pint) double cream and the seeds scraped from 1 vanilla pod in a saucepan and warm gently until the fudge has melted and the sauce is smooth. Leave to cool slightly. Meanwhile, place 6 crumbly oat cookies in a food processor and whizz until they form crumbs. Divide the crumbs between 4 tall sundae glasses, then add 1 scoop of vanilla or fudge ice cream to each. Drizzle over the fudge sauce and serve immediately.

Oat-Coated Fudge Cookies

Place 125 g (4 oz) softened unsalted butter and 75 g (3 oz) soft light brown sugar in a bowl and beat together with a hand-held electric whisk until light and fluffy. Add 1 large lightly beaten egg and 1 teaspoon vanilla extract and beat well. Stir in 225 g (7½ oz) plain flour, ½ teaspoon bicarbonate of soda and 50 g (2 oz) mini fudge chunks. Roll the mixture into 20–22 walnut-sized balls. Sprinkle 2–3 tablespoons rolled oats on to a plate and gently push the top of each ball into the oats, flattening slightly. Place on 2 baking sheets lined with nonstick baking paper and bake in a preheated oven, 200°C (400°F), Gas Mark 6, for 8–10 minutes until golden. Transfer to wire racks to cool.

1 ⏱ Peanut Butter Sandwich Cookies

Makes 8

2 tablespoons crunchy peanut butter

25 g (1 oz) unsalted butter, softened

1 tablespoon icing sugar, sifted

½ teaspoon vanilla bean paste

16 plain sweet biscuits

2 tablespoons seedless raspberry or strawberry jam

- Beat together the peanut butter, butter, icing sugar and vanilla paste in a small bowl.

- Spread the mixture over the back of 8 of the biscuits and top each with a dollop of the jam.

- Top with the remaining biscuits and sandwich together.

 Peanut Butter Cookies Place

Place 75 g (3 oz) unsalted butter and 75 g (3 oz) crunchy peanut butter in a saucepan over a low heat and warm gently until just melted. Sift 225 g (7½ oz) plain flour and ½ teaspoon bicarbonate of soda into a bowl. Add 100 g (3½ oz) soft light brown sugar, then stir in the melted butters and 1 large lightly beaten egg and mix until combined. Roll the mixture into 22–24 walnut-sized balls. Place, well spaced apart, on 2 large baking sheets lined with nonstick baking paper and flatten gently, then press the cookies with the back of a fork. Bake in a preheated oven, 200°C (400°F), Gas Mark 6, for 10–15 minutes until lightly golden. Transfer to wire racks to cool.

 Peanut Butter Pinwheel Cookies

Place 3 tablespoons blanched, unsalted peanuts in a dry frying pan and toast over a medium-low heat, stirring frequently, until golden. Tip on to a plate and leave to cool. Tip the peanuts into a mini chopper or food processor and pulse until finely chopped but not powdery. Roll out 350 g (11½ oz) pack chilled cookie dough to 25 x 15 cm (10 x 6 inches). Spread 2 tablespoons smooth or crunchy peanut butter evenly over the dough and sprinkle with the chopped peanuts. Roll up the dough lengthways into a sausage and cut into 12–14 x 1.5 cm (¾ inch) slices. Place, well spaced apart, on 2 baking sheets lined with nonstick baking paper

and bake in a preheated oven, 180°C (350°F), Gas Mark 4, for 12–14 minutes until lightly golden. Leave to cool on the sheets until firm, then transfer to wire racks to cool completely.

3. Gingerbread Men

Makes 12–14

75 g (3 oz) cold unsalted butter, diced
125 g (4 oz) plain wholemeal flour
125 g (4 oz) self-raising flour, plus extra for dusting
2 teaspoons ground ginger
½ teaspoon ground cinnamon
pinch of ground cloves
75 g (3 oz) soft light brown sugar
1 tablespoon black treacle
2 tablespoons golden syrup
1 small egg, lightly beaten
handful of currants, to decorate

- Line 2 baking sheets with nonstick baking paper. Place the butter, flours and spices in a food processor and pulse until the mixture resembles fine breadcrumbs. Add the sugar, treacle, golden syrup and egg and pulse until just combined.

- Tip the mixture on to a floured surface and knead gently until smooth. Roll out to 3 mm (⅛ inch) thick, then cut into 12–14 large gingerbread man shapes, rerolling the trimmings if necessary.

- Place the gingerbread men on the prepared baking sheets and press in currants for eyes. Bake in a preheated oven, 180°C (350°F), Gas Mark 4, for 15–18 minutes until golden. Leave to cool on the sheets for 2–3 minutes, then transfer to wire racks to cool completely.

---

1. Iced Gingerbread Men

Sift 125 g (4 oz) icing sugar into a bowl and add just enough milk to form a smooth, thick paste of piping consistency. Add 1–2 drops food colouring, then stir well. Spoon the icing into a piping bag fitted with a small icing nozzle, then use to pipe details on to 8–12 shop-bought gingerbread men. Decorate with edible coloured balls and sweeties, if liked, then leave to set.

2. Ginger Nut Biscuits

Place 100 g (3½ oz) unsalted butter and 125 g (4 oz) golden syrup in a small saucepan over a low heat and warm until just melted. Meanwhile, place 175 g (6 oz) granulated or demerara sugar in a bowl, then sift in 350 g (11½ oz) self-raising flour, 1 teaspoon bicarbonate of soda and 1 tablespoon ground ginger. Stir the melted butter into the dry ingredients and mix well. Roll the mixture into about 22 walnut-sized balls, adding 1–2 tablespoons milk if necessary. Place, well spaced apart, on 2 large baking sheets lined with nonstick baking paper and flatten slightly. Bake in a preheated oven, 200°C (400°F), Gas Mark 6, for 15 minutes, or until golden and cracked. Transfer to wire racks to cool.

Orangey Petticoat Tails

Makes 8

350 g (11½ oz) pack chilled cookie dough with orange or plain chocolate chunks

flour, for dusting

1–2 teaspoons orange-flavoured sugar or granulated sugar, for sprinkling (optional)

- Roll out the cookie dough on a floured surface to fit a 23 cm (9 inch) loose-bottomed fluted tart tin. Press gently into the tin so that the edge rises up slightly.

- Bake in a preheated oven, 180°C (350°F), Gas Mark 4, for 12–15 minutes, or according to the packet instructions, until golden. Using a sharp knife, carefully cut the cookie into 8 wedges while still in the tin. Prick the surface all over with a fork to resemble shortbread petticoat tails.

- Turn out of the tin, leaving the wedges on the loose tin base. Place on a wire rack and leave to cool. Serve sprinkled with the sugar, if liked.

1 Orange Curd Shortbreads

Place 50 g (2 oz) softened unsalted butter and 50 g (2 oz) sifted icing sugar in a bowl and beat together with a hand-held electric whisk until light and fluffy. Add 1 teaspoon grated orange rind and 1 tablespoon orange curd and beat until smooth. Spread the buttercream over 16 thin shortbread biscuits and top each with a second biscuit and sandwich together. Serve dusted with icing sugar.

3 Orangey Shortbread

Biscuits Place 150 g (5 oz) softened unsalted butter and 75 g (3 oz) caster sugar in a food processor and blend until smooth. Add 200 g (7 oz) plain flour and 2 teaspoons finely grated orange rind and pulse until just combined. Knead lightly until smooth, then roll into a sausage 20 cm (8 inches) long. Sprinkle 50 g (2 oz) granulated sugar on to a board, then roll the dough in the sugar to coat. Cut into 18–20 x 1 cm (½ inch) slices and place, well spaced apart, on 2 baking sheets lined with nonstick baking paper. Bake in a preheated oven, 200°C (400°F), Gas Mark 6, for 15 minutes, or until a pale golden colour. Transfer to a wire rack to cool.

30 Powdery Almond and Vanilla Crackles

Makes 24–26

100 g (3½ oz) plain flour
100 g (3½ oz) ground almonds
1 teaspoon bicarbonate of soda
200 g (7 oz) caster sugar
75 g (3 oz) unsalted butter,
  melted and cooled
1 large egg, lightly beaten
1 teaspoon vanilla bean paste
  or extract
50 g (2 oz) icing sugar

- Line 2 large baking sheets with nonstick baking paper. Place all of the ingredients except the icing sugar in a bowl and mix until smooth. Cover and chill for 10–15 minutes until firm.

- Sift the icing sugar into a separate bowl. Roll the dough into 24–26 walnut-sized balls, then roll them in the icing sugar to coat and place on the prepared baking sheets.

- Bake in a preheated oven, 200°C (400°F), Gas Mark 6, for 10–12 minutes until cracked and lightly golden. Leave to cool on the sheets for 1 minute, then transfer to wire racks to cool completely.

 Almond and Vanilla Croissants

Mix together 50 g (2 oz) coarsely grated marzipan, 2 tablespoons vanilla sugar, 2 tablespoons melted unsalted butter and 25 g (1 oz) plain dark chocolate chips in a bowl. Cut a slit horizontally into 4 croissants, then divide the mixture between the croissants. Place on a baking sheet and scatter over 25 g (1 oz) flaked almonds. Bake in a preheated oven, 200°C (400°F), Gas Mark 6, for 3–4 minutes until the almonds are pale golden and the chocolate is beginning to melt. Transfer to wire racks to cool slightly, then serve warm dusted with icing sugar.

 Almond and Vanilla Softs

Place 100 g (3½ oz) softened unsalted butter, 100 g (3½ oz) golden caster sugar and 1 teaspoon vanilla bean paste or extract in a bowl and beat together with a hand-held electric whisk until light and fluffy, then stir in 75 g (3 oz) ground almonds. Whisk 2 large egg whites in a clean bowl with a hand-held electric whisk until stiff, then fold gently into the almond mixture. Fold in 50 g (2 oz) plain flour. Drop about 15 small spoonfuls of the mixture on to 2 baking sheets lined with nonstick baking paper and dust generously with icing sugar.

Bake in a preheated oven, 220°C (425°F), Gas Mark 7, for 5–8 minutes until lightly golden. Leave on the sheets until firm, then transfer to wire racks to cool completely.

CAK-BISC-TOG

Cherry Coconut Drops

Makes 20–22

150 g (5 oz) unsalted butter, softened

125 g (4 oz) caster sugar

½ teaspoon almond extract

1 large egg plus 1 large egg yolk, lightly beaten

75 g (3 oz) desiccated coconut

100 g (3½ oz) plain flour

10–12 glacé cherries, halved

- Line 2 baking sheets with nonstick baking paper. Place the butter, sugar and almond extract in a large bowl and beat together with a hand-held electric whisk until light and fluffy. Add the egg and egg yolk and beat well. Add the coconut and flour and stir until combined.

- Drop 20–22 heaped teaspoonfuls of the mixture on to the prepared baking sheets and top each one with a halved glacé cherry.

- Bake in a preheated oven, 200°C (400°F), Gas Mark 6, for 10–12 minutes until lightly golden. Leave to cool on the sheets for 2–3 minutes, then transfer to wire racks to cool completely.

 Cherry Coconut Meringue Sundaes

Place 4 generous scoops of coconut-flavoured ice cream in 4 tall sundae glasses. Divide 200 g (7 oz) drained canned black cherries in syrup between the glasses, then crumble 1 meringue nest over each. Serve immediately.

 Chewy Coconut Meringues

Using a hand-held electric whisk, whisk 3 large egg whites in a large, clean bowl until they form soft peaks, then gradually whisk in 250 g (8 oz) caster sugar, beating well between each addition, until the mixture is thick and glossy. Gently fold in

200 g (7 oz) desiccated coconut and 1 teaspoon almond extract. Drop about 24 small spoonfuls of the meringue mixture on to 2 baking sheets lined with nonstick baking paper. Bake in a preheated oven, 180°C (350°F), Gas Mark 4, for 18–20 minutes until lightly golden. Transfer to wire racks to cool.

CAK-BISC-QIJ

30 Spiced Hazelnut Palmiers

Makes 30–40

50 g (2 oz) whole blanched
   hazelnuts
1½ teaspoons ground cinnamon
¼ teaspoon ground nutmeg
¾ teaspoon ground ginger
3 tablespoons demerara sugar
375 g (12 oz) chilled ready-rolled
   puff pastry
50 g (2 oz) unsalted butter,
   melted
icing sugar, for dusting

- Line 2 large baking sheets with nonstick baking paper. Put the hazelnuts in a large, dry frying pan and toast over a medium-low heat for 4–5 minutes, shaking frequently, until lightly toasted. Tip into a food processor with the spices and blend until finely chopped. Place the sugar in a bowl and stir in the nuts.

- Unroll the pastry on a clean surface and brush lightly with some of the melted butter. Sprinkle over the nut mixture, then roll the long sides of the pastry into the centre. Cut into 30–40 x 1 cm (½ inch) slices and place on the prepared baking sheets. Brush with the remaining butter.

- Bake in a preheated oven, 220°C (425°F), Gas Mark 7, for 10 minutes, then remove from the oven and turn the palmiers over. Return to the oven and cook for a further 5–8 minutes until puffed up and golden. Transfer to wire racks to cool. Serve dusted with icing sugar.

1 Spiced Sugar Puffs

Unroll 375 g (12 oz) chilled ready-rolled puff pastry, then brush with 50 g (2 oz) melted unsalted butter and cut into 20 x 2 cm (¾ inch) strips. Place on 2 large baking sheets lined with nonstick baking paper and bake in a preheated oven, 230°C (450°F), Gas Mark 8, for 7–8 minutes until puffed and golden. Meanwhile, sift together 3 tablespoons icing sugar and 1 teaspoon ground mixed spice in a small bowl. Transfer the puffs to a wire rack and dust with the spiced sugar.

2 Spiced Puff Torsades

Mix together 50 g (2 oz) chopped toasted hazelnuts, 3 tablespoons golden caster sugar and 2 teaspoons ground mixed spice in a bowl. Unroll 375 g (12 oz) chilled ready-rolled puff pastry, then brush with 50 g (2 oz) melted unsalted butter and sprinkle with the nut mixture. Fold the pastry in half lengthways and cut into about 30 x 1.5 cm (¾ inch) strips. Twist each strip and place on 2 large baking sheets lined with nonstick baking paper. Bake in a preheated oven, 220°C (425°F), Gas Mark 7, for 12–15 minutes until puffed and golden. Transfer to wire racks to cool slightly, then serve warm dusted with icing sugar.

1 ⏱ Digestive-Coated Ice Cream Sandwiches

Makes 4

8 plain digestive biscuits
8 chocolate-coated digestive
biscuits
4 scoops of soft honeycomb or
vanilla ice cream

- Place the plain digestive biscuits in a freezer bag and tap with a rolling pin until evenly crushed. Tip on to a plate.

- Place 1 scoop of ice cream on each of 4 of the chocolate-coated biscuits, shaping the ice cream so that it makes a circle the same size as the biscuit. Top with the remaining chocolate-coated biscuits and sandwich together.

- Roll the ice cream in the crushed biscuits until coated. Serve immediately or place on a baking sheet, cover and freeze until required.

---

2 ◗ Choc and Nut Digestives

Melt 100 g (3½ oz) milk or plain dark chocolate, broken into small pieces, in a heatproof bowl set over a saucepan of gently simmering water, ensuring the bowl does not touch the water. Melt 50 g (2 oz) white chocolate in the same way. Once the dark chocolate has melted, brush over one side of 12 digestive biscuits. Place the biscuits on a baking sheet, then sprinkle with 50 g (2 oz) flaked or chopped toasted nuts and drizzle with the melted white chocolate. Chill for 8–10 minutes, or until the chocolate has set.

3 ◗ Classic Digestive Sweetmeals

Place 150 g (5 oz) wholemeal flour, 75 g (3 oz) oat bran, a pinch of salt, 1 scant teaspoon baking powder and 75 g (3 oz) soft light brown sugar in a bowl and mix until combined. Add 125 g (4 oz) softened unsalted butter and rub in with the fingertips until the mixture resembles fine breadcrumbs, then add enough of 1–2 tablespoons milk to make a firm dough. Roll out on a floured surface to 4 mm (¼ inch) thick, then stamp out 12–14 rounds using a 7 cm (3 inch) plain cutter. Place on 2 baking sheets lined with nonstick baking paper and bake in a preheated oven, 200°C (400°F), Gas Mark 6, for 15 minutes, or until lightly golden. Transfer to wire racks to cool.

2 Banoffee Chip Bites

Makes about 25

50 g (2 oz) sweetened dried
   banana chips
150 g (5 oz) plain flour, plus extra
   for dusting
100 g (3½ oz) rolled oats
50 g (2 oz) baking fudge chunks
150 g (5 oz) caster sugar
125 g (4 oz) unsalted butter
2 tablespoons dulce de leche or
   thick caramel sauce
1 teaspoon bicarbonate of soda
1 tablespoon boiling water

- Line 2 baking sheets with nonstick baking paper. Place the banana chips in a freezer bag and tap lightly with a rolling pin to break them up, but not crush completely. Tip into a bowl, then add the flour, oats, fudge chunks and sugar and mix until combined.

- Place the butter and dulce de leche or caramel sauce in a small saucepan over a low heat and warm until just melted. Put the bicarbonate of soda in a small bowl and stir in the boiling water. Add to the melted butter, then stir into the dry ingredients.

- Use lightly floured hands to roll the mixture into about 25 walnut-sized balls, then place on the prepared baking sheets.

- Bake in a preheated oven, 200°C (400°F), Gas Mark 6, for 10 minutes, or until golden. Leave to cool on the sheets until firm, then transfer to wire racks to cool completely.

---

1 Quick Banoffee Cookie Pies

Place 12 Oreo-style cookies in a freezer bag and tap with a rolling pin until evenly crushed. Spoon all but 1 tablespoon of the crushed biscuits into 4 glass serving dishes and pour 1 tablespoon dulce de leche or thick caramel sauce over each. Top with 2 small, sliced bananas and finish with a dollop of whipped cream. Sprinkle with the reserved crushed biscuits and serve immediately.

3 Banoffee Cookies

Place 100 g (3½ oz) soft light brown sugar, 125 g (4 oz) softened unsalted butter and 2 tablespoons dulce de leche or thick caramel sauce in a bowl and beat together with a hand-held electric whisk until pale and creamy. Add 1 large lightly beaten egg and beat well. Break up 75 g (3 oz) sweetened dried banana chips in a freezer bag as above. Add 50 g (2 oz) of the chips to the butter mixture with 225 g (7½ oz) plain flour and 1 teaspoon bicarbonate of soda and mix to form a soft dough. Use floured hands to roll the dough into 12–16 walnut-sized balls, then place on 2 baking sheets lined with nonstick baking paper and flatten slightly. Using your fingertip, make a dip in each cookie and fill with 1 scant teaspoon dulce de leche or thick caramel sauce. Sprinkle over the remaining banana chips and bake in a preheated oven, 200°C (400°F), Gas Mark 6, for 10–12 minutes until golden. Transfer to wire racks to cool.

30 Chopped Nut Snickerdoodles

Makes 18–22

125 g (4 oz) unsalted butter, softened

1 teaspoon vanilla bean paste or extract

200 g (7 oz) golden caster sugar

1 large egg, lightly beaten

50 g (2 oz) chopped nuts

200 g (7 oz) plain flour

1 teaspoon cream of tartar

½ teaspoon baking powder

2 teaspoons ground cinnamon

pinch of ground nutmeg

¼ teaspoon salt

- Line 2 baking sheets with nonstick baking paper. Place the butter, vanilla paste or extract and 150 g (5 oz) of the sugar in a bowl and beat together with a hand-held electric whisk until light and fluffy. Add the egg and beat well, then stir in the chopped nuts. Sift in the flour, cream of tartar, baking powder, 1 teaspoon of the cinnamon, the nutmeg and salt and stir until combined.

- Mix the remaining cinnamon and sugar in a small bowl and sprinkle over a plate. Roll the dough into 18–22 walnut-sized balls, then roll them in the cinnamon sugar to coat. Place, well spaced apart, on the prepared baking sheets and flatten slightly.

- Bake in a preheated oven, 200°C (400°F), Gas Mark 6, for 12–15 minutes until firm. Leave to cool on the baking sheets for 2 minutes, then transfer to wire racks to cool completely.

10 Cinnamon Nut Creams

Place 100 g (3½ oz) sifted icing sugar, 50 g (2 oz) softened unsalted butter, 1 teaspoon ground cinnamon and ½ teaspoon vanilla bean paste in a bowl and beat together with a hand-held electric whisk until smooth, then stir in 50 g (2 oz) chopped toasted nuts. Spread the buttercream over 20 ginger nut biscuits, place another biscuit on top of each and sandwich together.

20 Nut Cluster Cookies

Place 125 g (4 oz) roughly chopped mixed nuts, such as pecans, pistachios, roasted hazelnuts and flaked almonds, 175 g (6 oz) soft light brown sugar, 75 g (3 oz) golden caster sugar and 225 g (7½ oz) sifted self-raising flour in a large bowl. Whisk together 125 g (4 oz) melted and cooled unsalted butter, 1 large lightly beaten egg and 1 teaspoon almond extract in a jug. Pour into the dry ingredients and mix to form a soft dough. Roll the dough into about 25 walnut-sized balls, then place on 2 baking sheets lined with nonstick baking paper and flatten slightly. Bake in a preheated oven, 200°C (400°F), Gas Mark 6, for 8–10 minutes until golden. Leave to cool on the baking sheets for 1 minute, then transfer to wire racks to cool completely.

Chocolate Viennese Whirls

Makes about 15

200 g (7 oz) unsalted butter, softened

50 g (2 oz) icing sugar, sifted

125 g (4 oz) self-raising flour

2 tablespoons good-quality cocoa powder

4 tablespoons cornflour

1–3 teaspoons milk

- Line 2 baking sheets with nonstick baking paper. Place the butter and icing sugar in a bowl and beat together using a hand-held electric whisk until light and fluffy. Sift in the flour, cocoa powder and cornflour and mix to a smooth paste, adding just enough of the milk to form a piping consistency.

- Spoon the mixture into a piping bag fitted with a star-shaped nozzle, then pipe about 15 whirls on to the prepared baking sheets.

- Bake in a preheated oven, 200°C (400°F), Gas Mark 6, for 8–10 minutes until firm. Leave to cool on the sheets for 1 minute, then transfer to wire racks to cool completely.

Chocolate-Dipped Viennese Whirls

Melt 100 g (3½ oz) plain dark chocolate, broken into small pieces, in a heatproof bowl set over a saucepan of gently simmering water, ensuring the bowl does not touch the water. Dip a shop-bought Viennese whirl halfway in the melted chocolate and place on a baking sheet lined with nonstick baking paper. Repeat with a further 10–12 biscuits, then place in the freezer for 3–5 minutes until the chocolate is just set. Serve with Viennese-style hot chocolate.

Chocolate Cream Viennese Whirls

Make the Viennese whirls as above, then leave to cool. Meanwhile, place 50 g (2 oz) softened unsalted butter, 100 g (3½ oz) icing sugar and 2 tablespoons chocolate spread in a bowl and beat together with a hand-held electric whisk until smooth. Once the whirls are cool, spread the chocolate cream over half the whirls, then sandwich together with the remaining biscuits.

30 Giant C'raisin Cookies

Makes 8–10

150 g (5 oz) unsalted butter,
  softened
225 g (7½ oz) golden caster sugar
1 large egg, lightly beaten
¼ teaspoon orange extract
  (optional)
50 g (2 oz) dried cranberries
75 g (3 oz) raisins
250 g (8 oz) plain flour
1 teaspoon bicarbonate of soda

· Line 2 baking sheets with nonstick baking paper. Place the butter and sugar in a large bowl and beat together using a hand-held electric whisk until light and fluffy. Add the egg and orange extract, if using, and beat well. Stir in the cranberries and raisins, then sift in the flour and bicarbonate of soda and mix to form a stiff mixture.

· Place 8–10 mounds of the mixture, well spaced apart and without flattening, on the prepared baking sheets.

· Bake in a preheated oven, 200°C (400°F), Gas Mark 6, for 12–15 minutes, or until pale golden. Leave to cool on the sheets for 2–3 minutes, then transfer to wire racks to cool completely.

 Iced C'raisin Cookies

Mix 75 g (3 oz) sifted icing sugar with just enough cranberry juice to form a smooth icing of piping consistency. Place 12 sweet oat biscuits on a baking sheet, then drizzle over the icing and scatter 25 g (1 oz) each of cranberries and raisins over the top. Chill for 5–8 minutes to set the icing.

 Mini C'raisin Clusters

Place 100 g (3½ oz) melted unsalted butter in a bowl and stir in 100 ml (3½ fl oz) maple syrup. Whisk in 1 large lightly beaten egg, then stir in 75 g (3 oz) toasted nut muesli, 50 g (2 oz) each of dried cranberries and raisins and 150 g (5 oz) plain flour. Place about 20 small spoonfuls of the mixture on 2 large baking sheets lined with nonstick baking paper and flatten with the back of the spoon. Bake in a preheated oven, 200°C (400°F), Gas Mark 6, for 10 minutes, or until golden. Transfer to wire racks to cool.

20 Figgy Anzac Biscuits

Makes 28–30

150 g (5 oz) plain flour
100 g (3½ oz) rolled oats
50 g (2 oz) desiccated coconut
75 g (3 oz) ready-to-eat
  semi-dried figs, chopped
175 g (6 oz) golden caster sugar
125 g (4 oz) unsalted butter
2 tablespoons golden syrup
1 teaspoon bicarbonate of soda
1 tablespoon boiling water

- Line 2 large baking sheets with nonstick baking paper. Mix together the flour, oats, coconut, figs and sugar in a large bowl.

- Place the butter and golden syrup in a small saucepan over a low heat and warm until just melted. Put the bicarbonate of soda in a small bowl and stir in the boiling water. Add to the melted butter, then stir into the dry ingredients.

- Use lightly floured hands to roll the mixture into 28–30 walnut-sized balls, then place on the prepared baking sheets.

- Bake in a preheated oven, 200°C (400°F), Gas Mark 6, for 10–12 minutes until golden. Transfer to wire racks to cool.

10 Figgy Oat Muesli

Place 200 g (7 oz) rolled oats, 2 tablespoons sunflower seeds and 3 tablespoons wheat bran on a baking sheet and bake in a preheated oven, 220°C (425°F), Gas Mark 7, for 5–6 minutes until pale golden. Tip into a large bowl and leave to cool for 2–3 minutes, then stir in 100 g (3½ oz) chopped ready-to-eat semi-dried figs, 50 g (2 oz) raisins, 25 g (1 oz) dried banana chips and 75 g (3 oz) cornflakes or puffed rice. Mix well and serve with cold milk or yogurt.

30 Figgy Oat Cookies

Mix together 75 g (3 oz) chopped ready-to-eat semi-dried figs, 50 g (2 oz) desiccated coconut, 200 g (7 oz) wholemeal self-raising flour, 125 g (4 oz) soft dark brown sugar, 25 g (1 oz) cornflakes and 75 g (3 oz) rolled oats in a large bowl. Place 125 g (4 oz) unsalted butter and 2 tablespoons golden syrup in a small saucepan over a low heat and warm until just melted. Add to the dry ingredients with 1 large lightly beaten egg and mix until combined. Roll about 18 large spoonfuls of the mixture into golf ball-sized balls. Place, well spaced apart, on 2 baking sheets lined with nonstick baking paper and flatten with a wide palette knife or your fingertips. Bake in a preheated oven, 200°C (400°F), Gas Mark 6, for 12–15 minutes until golden. Leave to cool on the sheets for 1–2 minutes, then transfer to wire racks to harden.

30 Cappuccino Cookies

Makes about 20

225 g (7½ oz) unsalted butter, softened

75 g (3 oz) icing sugar, sifted

½ teaspoon vanilla bean paste or extract

200 g (7 oz) plain flour

4 tablespoons cornflour

1–2 tablespoons milk

1 tablespoon cocoa powder

1 teaspoon coffee essence

hot chocolate powder, for dusting

- Line 2 large baking sheets with nonstick baking paper. Place the butter, icing sugar and vanilla bean paste or extract in a bowl and beat together with a hand-held electric whisk until light and fluffy. Sift in the flour and cornflour and stir until smooth, adding just enough of the milk to form a dough of piping consistency.

- Place half of the mixture in a second bowl, sift in the cocoa powder and fold in until combined. Stir the coffee essence into the first bowl until evenly combined.

- Spoon the cocoa mixture into one side of a piping bag fitted with a star-shaped nozzle, and the coffee-flavoured mixture into the other side so that both mixtures will be piped out at the same time. Pipe about 20 whirls or other shapes on to the prepared baking sheets.

- Bake in a preheated oven, 200°C (400°F), Gas Mark 6, for 10–15 minutes until lightly golden. Transfer to wire racks to cool. Serve dusted with chocolate powder.

 Cappuccino Moments

Place 100 g (3½ oz) mascarpone cheese, 75 g (3 oz) sifted icing sugar and 2 teaspoons coffee essence in a bowl and beat until smooth. Spread the mixture thickly over 18 chocolate cookies, then decorate with white and plain dark chocolate curls. Serve immediately or chill until required.

 Cappuccino Crispies

Place 200 g (7 oz) plain flour and 125 g (4 oz) cold, diced unsalted butter in a food processor and pulse until the mixture resembles fine breadcrumbs. Add 125 g (4 oz) demerara sugar and 1 tablespoon cocoa powder and pulse once. Add 1 large lightly beaten egg and 1 teaspoon coffee essence and pulse briefly until the mixture forms a soft dough, adding 1–2 teaspoons milk if necessary. Tip on to a floured surface and shape into a 30 x 5 x 2.5 cm (12 x 2 x 1 inch) flat log. Cut into about 30 x 1 cm (½ inch) slices and place on 2 large baking sheets lined with nonstick baking paper. Sprinkle with 2 tablespoons demerara sugar and bake in a preheated oven, 200°C (400°F), Gas Mark 6, for 10–15 minutes until golden. Transfer to wire racks to cool.

30 Really Chocolatey Choc Chunk Cookies

Makes 14–16

125 g (4 oz) unsalted butter, softened

100 g (3 oz) caster sugar

1 large egg, lightly beaten

50 g (2 oz) hazelnut chocolate spread

½ teaspoon vanilla bean paste or extract (optional)

150 g (5 oz) plain flour

1½ tablespoons cocoa powder

½ teaspoon bicarbonate of soda

½ teaspoon baking powder

100 g (3½ oz) milk or plain dark chocolate, cut into chunks

75 g (3 oz) white chocolate, cut into chunks

50 g (2 oz) mini sugar-coated, coloured chocolate buttons

- Line 2 baking sheets with nonstick baking paper. Place the butter and sugar in a large bowl and beat together using a hand-held electric whisk until light and fluffy. Add the egg, chocolate spread and vanilla paste or extract, if using, and beat well. Sift in the flour, cocoa powder, bicarbonate of soda and baking powder, then add the chocolate chunks and stir until the mixture is smooth.

- Drop 14–16 small spoonfuls of the mixture on to the prepared baking sheets and scatter the mini chocolate buttons on top.

- Bake in a preheated oven, 200°C (400°F), Gas Mark 6, for 12–14 minutes until slightly firm around the edges. Transfer to wire racks to cool.

 Chocolate Bourbons

Beat together 2 tablespoons hazelnut chocolate spread, 50 g (2 oz) softened unsalted butter, 125 g (4 oz) icing sugar and 1 tablespoon white chocolate chips or strands in a bowl. Spread the buttercream over 30 thin chocolate biscuits and sandwich together.

 Easy Choc Chunk Cookies

Place 100 g (3½ oz) unsalted butter and 2 tablespoons hazelnut chocolate spread in a small saucepan over a low heat and warm until just melted. Sift 175 g (6 oz) plain flour, 2 tablespoons cocoa powder and ½ teaspoon bicarbonate of soda into a large bowl, then stir in 100 g (3½ oz) golden caster sugar. Stir the melted butter into the dry ingredients with 1 large lightly beaten egg and 75 g (3 oz) each of white and milk or plain dark chocolate chips. Roll the mixture into 20–22 walnut-sized balls, then place on 2 large baking sheets lined with nonstick baking paper and flatten slightly. Bake in a preheated oven, 200°C (400°F), Gas Mark 6, for 10–12 minutes until slightly firm around the edges. Transfer to wire racks to cool.

30 Clove and Cardamom Spice Cookies

Makes 30–40

175 g (6 oz) unsalted butter, softened

200 g (7 oz) soft dark brown sugar

1 large egg, lightly beaten

½ teaspoon ground cinnamon

¼ teaspoon ground cardamom (or the ground seeds from 3 pods)

¼ teaspoon ground cloves

325 g (11 oz) plain flour, plus extra for dusting

1 teaspoon baking powder

½ teaspoon salt

- Line 3 baking sheets with nonstick baking paper. Place the butter and sugar in a large bowl and beat together with a hand-held electric whisk until light and fluffy. Add the egg and spices and beat well. Stir in the flour, baking powder and salt and mix until combined.

- Turn the dough out on to a floured surface and knead lightly until smooth. Roll out to 2–3 mm (⅛ inch) thick, then cut out about 30–40 shapes, such as stars, or stamp out rounds using a 6 cm (2½ inch) fluted cutter.

- Place the cookies on the prepared baking sheets and bake in a preheated oven, 180°C (350°F), Gas Mark 4, for 14–16 minutes until lightly golden and tinged brown around the edges. Transfer to wire racks to cool.

---

1 Clove and Cardamom Custard Creams Place 50 g (2 oz) softened unsalted butter, 75 g (3 oz) sifted icing sugar, 1 tablespoon custard powder and 1 pinch each of ground cinnamon, ground cardamom and ground cloves in a bowl and beat together with a hand-held electric whisk until smooth. Spread the buttercream over 30 thin shortbread biscuits, place another biscuit on top of each and sandwich together.

2 Clove and Cardamom Kisses Place 175 g (6 oz) softened unsalted butter, 75 g (3 oz) sifted icing sugar and 1 large lightly beaten egg in a bowl and beat together with a hand-held electric whisk until pale and creamy. Sift in 100 g (3½ oz) self-raising flour, 50 g (2 oz) cornflour, ½ teaspoon ground cinnamon, ¼ teaspoon ground cardamom and ¼ teaspoon ground cloves and mix to a smooth paste. Spoon the mixture into a piping bag fitted with a star-shaped nozzle, then pipe 16–20 small whirls on to 2 baking sheets lined with nonstick baking paper. Bake in a preheated oven, 200°C (400°F), Gas Mark 6, for 10 minutes, or until golden. Leave to cool on the sheets for 1 minute, then transfer to wire racks to cool completely.

2 Nutty Florentine Bites

Makes about 24

100 ml (3½ fl oz) sweetened
   condensed milk
25 g (1 oz) cornflakes
50 g (2 oz) flaked almonds
25 g (1 oz) glacé cherries,
   chopped
25 g (1 oz) pecan nuts, chopped
25 g (1 oz) macadamia nuts or
   blanched, unsalted peanuts,
   chopped

- Line 2 x 12-hole nonstick mini muffin tins with paper mini muffin cases or lightly grease, or line 2 large baking sheets with nonstick baking paper.

- Put the condensed milk in a saucepan over a low heat and warm through, then remove from the heat and stir in the remaining ingredients.

- Drop about 24 small spoonfuls of the mixture into the prepared mini muffin tins or on to the baking sheets.

- Bake in a preheated oven, 180°C (350°F), Gas Mark 4, for 10–12 minutes until golden. Leave to cool in the tins until hardened, then transfer to a wire rack to cool completely.

---

1 Chocolate Florentine Toppers

Melt 75 g (3 oz) white chocolate, broken into small pieces, in a heatproof bowl set over a saucepan of gently simmering water, ensuring the bowl does not touch the water, then leave to cool slightly. Meanwhile, mix together 50 g (2 oz) flaked almonds and 25 g (1 oz) each of chopped pecans, chopped macadamia nuts or blanched peanuts and chopped glacé cherries in a bowl. Place 15 plain butter biscuits on a baking sheet and spread with the melted chocolate. Scatter over the nut mixture, then leave in a cool place for a few minutes until the chocolate has set.

3 Florentine Cookies

Place 75 g (3 oz) softened unsalted butter and 150 g (5 oz) golden caster sugar in a large bowl and beat together with a hand-held electric whisk until light and fluffy. Beat together 1 large egg plus 1 large egg yolk in a jug and gradually add to the butter mixture, beating well between each addition. Stir in 25 g (1 oz) each of chopped pecan nuts, chopped macadamia nuts or peanuts and chopped glacé cherries. Sift in 175 g (6 oz) self-raising flour and ½ teaspoon bicarbonate of soda and stir until smooth. Roll the mixture into about 16–20 walnut-sized balls, adding a little extra flour if necessary. Place on 2 baking sheets lined with nonstick baking paper and flatten slightly. Bake in a preheated oven, 200°C (400°F), Gas Mark 6, for 10–12 minutes until golden. Leave to cool on the sheets for 1 minute, then transfer to wire racks to cool completely.

Chocolate Orange Cookies

Makes 20–22

125 g (4 oz) unsalted butter, softened
125 g (4 oz) demerara sugar
1 teaspoon finely grated orange rind
1 teaspoon orange extract
1 large egg, lightly beaten
150 g (5 oz) plain flour
½ teaspoon baking powder
½ teaspoon salt
75 g (3 oz) chocolate chips

- Line 2 large baking sheets with nonstick baking paper. Place the butter, sugar, orange rind and orange extract in a bowl and beat together with a hand-held electric whisk until light and fluffy. Add the egg and beat well, then sift in the flour, baking powder and salt. Add the chocolate chips and mix until combined.

- Drop 20–22 small spoonfuls of the mixture, well spaced apart, on to the prepared baking sheets.

- Bake in a preheated oven, 200°C (400°F), Gas Mark 6, for 10 minutes, or until golden. Transfer to wire racks to cool.

 Chocolate Orange Drizzle Biscuits

Melt 75 g (3 oz) orange-flavoured milk or plain dark chocolate, broken into small pieces, in a heatproof bowl set over a pan of gently simmering water, ensuring the bowl does not touch the water. Meanwhile, place 20 plain butter biscuits on a large baking sheet. Drizzle teaspoonfuls of the melted chocolate over the biscuits, then chill until the chocolate has set.

 Orange Butter Biscuits

Place 150 g (5 oz) softened unsalted butter, 75 g (3 oz) caster sugar, 1 teaspoon finely grated orange rind and 1 teaspoon orange extract in a large bowl and beat together with a hand-held electric whisk until light and fluffy. Add 1 large lightly beaten egg and beat well. Sift in 250 g (8 oz) plain flour and 2 tablespoons cornflour and mix to form a soft dough. Roll out on a floured surface to 3 mm (⅛ inch) thick, then stamp out about 25 rounds using a 7 cm (3 inch) plain or fluted cutter. Place on 2 baking sheets lined with nonstick baking paper and bake in a preheated oven, 200°C (400°F), Gas Mark 6, for 15 minutes, or until lightly golden. Transfer to wire racks to cool.

10 Sweetie Jar Moments

Makes 18

6 tablespoons chocolate spread
   or good-quality jam
18 plain biscuits, such as butter
   biscuits or shortbread
50 g (2 oz) mini marshmallows
mixture of small sweeties,
   to decorate

- Spread about 1 teaspoon of the chocolate spread or jam over 9 of the biscuits and top with the mini marshmallows.

- Slide under a preheated low grill for 1–2 minutes until the marshmallows are beginning to turn golden. Transfer to a wire rack to cool.

- Meanwhile, spread the remaining chocolate spread or jam over the remaining biscuits and decorate with the sweeties.

2 Sweetie Jar Gems

Place 100 g (3½ oz) softened unsalted butter and 75 g (3 oz) caster sugar in a large bowl and beat together with a hand-held electric whisk until light and fluffy. Add 1 large egg yolk and beat well. Add 175 g (6 oz) self-raising flour and mix to form a smooth dough. Roll out on a floured surface to 3 mm (⅛ inch) thick, then stamp out about 25 small flower- or other shaped biscuits and place on 2 large baking sheets lined with nonstick baking paper. Bake in a preheated oven, 200°C (400°F), Gas Mark 6, for 10 minutes, or until lightly golden. Transfer to wire racks to cool.

Once cool, pipe 2–3 tablespoons shop-bought coloured buttercream icing in little flower shapes on to the biscuits and top each with a small sweetie.

3 Sweetie Jar Biscuits

Place 75 g (3 oz) softened unsalted butter and 150 g (5 oz) caster sugar in a bowl and beat together with a hand-held electric whisk until light and fluffy. Gradually add 1 large egg and 1 large egg yolk and beat well. Sift in 200 g (7 oz) self-raising flour and ½ teaspoon bicarbonate of soda and mix until smooth. Drop about 18 dessertspoonfuls of the mixture on to 2 baking sheets lined with nonstick baking paper. Bake in a preheated oven, 200°C (400°F), Gas Mark 6, for 12–15 minutes. Transfer to wire racks to cool, then decorate as above.

30 White Chocolate and Macadamia Cookies

Makes 14–16

150 g (5 oz) unsalted butter, softened

225 g (7½ oz) caster sugar

1 large egg, lightly beaten

2 tablespoons milk

1 teaspoon vanilla bean paste or extract (optional)

75 g (3 oz) white chocolate chips

75 g (3 oz) macadamia nuts, roughly chopped

250 g (8 oz) plain flour

1 teaspoon bicarbonate of soda

- Line 2 baking sheets with nonstick baking paper. Place the butter and sugar in a bowl and beat together using a hand-held electric whisk until light and fluffy. Add the egg, milk and vanilla bean paste or extract, if using, and beat well. Stir in the chocolate chips and macadamia nuts, then sift in the flour and bicarbonate of soda and mix gently to form a soft dough.

- Drop 14–16 small spoonfuls of the dough, well spaced apart, on to the prepared baking sheets.

- Bake in a preheated oven, 200°C (400°F), Gas Mark 6, for 12–15 minutes until pale golden. Leave to cool on the sheets for 2–3 minutes, the transfer to wire racks to cool completely.

 White Choc and Macadamia

Toppers Melt 75 g (3 oz) white chocolate, broken into small pieces, in a heatproof bowl set over a saucepan of gently simmering water, ensuring the bowl does not touch the water. Meanwhile, place 12–16 rich tea biscuits on a baking sheet. Stir 100 g (3½ oz) halved macadamia nuts and 100 g (3½ oz) golden raisins into the chocolate, then spoon on to the biscuits. Freeze for 5 minutes, or until the chocolate has just set.

 Macadamia and Pecan Drops

Place 125 g (4 oz) softened unsalted butter, 1 teaspoon vanilla extract, 1 large lightly beaten egg and 225 g (7½ oz) soft light brown sugar in a bowl and beat together using a hand-held electric whisk. Sift in 225 g (7½ oz) plain flour, 1 teaspoon bicarbonate of soda and ½ teaspoon baking powder. Add 50 g (2 oz) each of roughly chopped macadamia and pecan nuts and 50 g (2 oz) baking fudge chunks and stir until

combined. Drop about 25 small mounds of the mixture, well spaced apart, on to 2 large baking sheets lined with nonstick baking paper. Bake in a preheated oven, 200°C (400°F), Gas Mark 6, for 8–10 minutes until golden. Leave to cool on the sheets for 1 minute, then transfer to wire racks to cool.

30 Lemony Sponge Fingers

Makes 14–16

2 large eggs, separated
75 g (3 oz) caster sugar
1½ teaspoons finely grated
  lemon rind
pinch of salt
75 g (3 oz) plain flour
icing sugar, to dust

- Line 2 baking sheets with nonstick baking paper. Place the egg yolks and half the sugar in a large bowl and beat with a hand-held electric whisk for 5–8 minutes until the mixture is pale and thick and the whisk leaves a trail when lifted above the mixture. Beat in the lemon rind and set aside.

- Whisk the egg whites in a clean bowl with a clean hand-held electric whisk until they form soft peaks, then gradually whisk in the remaining sugar and the salt. Fold the egg whites into the egg yolk mixture, then sift in the plain flour and fold in.

- Spoon the mixture into a piping bag fitted with a 1 cm (½ inch) plain nozzle, then pipe 14–16 x 7 cm (3 inch) lengths on to the prepared baking sheets.

- Bake in a preheated oven, 200°C (400°F), Gas Mark 6, for 10 minutes, or until pale golden. Transfer to wire racks to cool. Dust with icing sugar to serve.

---

1 **Lemon Sponge Mousses**

Cut 12 shop-bought sponge fingers in half and arrange around the edge of 4 serving dishes, so that the curved side is facing out. Gently spoon a 75 g (3 oz) pot lemon mousse into the centre of each one. Top with a dollop of whipped cream and scatter over a small handful of lightly toasted flaked almonds. Cover and chill until required.

2 **Lemon Buttons**
Sift 200 g (7 oz) plain flour and ½ teaspoon bicarbonate of soda into a large bowl. Stir in 100 g (3½ oz) caster sugar and 1½ teaspoons finely grated lemon rind, then add 150 g (5 oz) melted unsalted butter and 1 large lightly beaten egg and mix until combined. Drop about 25 small spoonfuls of the mixture, well spaced apart, on to 2 large baking sheets lined with nonstick baking paper. Bake in a preheated oven, 200°C (400°F), Gas Mark 6, for 10–15 minutes until lightly golden. Transfer to wire racks to cool.

QuickCook
Pies, Tarts and Puddings

Recipes listed by cooking time

10

 # Strawberry Ricotta Tartlets

Serves 6

6 sheets of feuilles de brick
    pastry
50 g (2 oz) unsalted butter,
    melted
2 tablespoons caster sugar
125 g (4 oz) strawberries, hulled
    and sliced

For the ricotta cream

250 g (8 oz) ricotta cheese
50 g (2 oz) icing sugar, sifted
1 teaspoon vanilla bean paste
    or the seeds scraped from
    1 vanilla pod
125 ml (4 fl oz) double cream

- Lay 1 sheet of pastry on a clean surface and brush with melted butter. Fold the 4 sides towards the centre of the pastry to form a square, then brush with more butter and push into a 200 ml (7 fl oz) metal pudding mould so that the pastry folds and forms 4 'petals'. Repeat with the remaining sheets of pastry to fill 6 moulds. Brush with any remaining butter and sprinkle each one with caster sugar.

- Place the moulds on a baking sheet and bake in a preheated oven, 220°C (425°F), Gas Mark 7, for 7–8 minutes until crisp and light golden.

- Meanwhile, make the ricotta cream. Place all the ingredients in a bowl and beat together with a hand-held electric whisk until thick and smooth.

- Remove the tart cases from the moulds and transfer to a wire rack to cool for 2–3 minutes. Spoon the filling into the pastry cases and decorate with the sliced strawberries. Serve immediately.

 Strawberry Ricotta Flan

Make the ricotta cream as above, then spread over 1 large sponge flan base and top with 250 g (8 oz) hulled and halved strawberries. Serve drizzled with 2 tablespoons runny honey or maple syrup.

 Strawberry Ricotta Pie

Place 200 g (7 oz) shop-bought sweet pastry cases in a freezer bag and tap lightly with a rolling pin until crushed. Tip into a bowl and mix with 50 g (2 oz) melted unsalted butter until well coated. Tip into a lightly greased 23 cm (9 inch) tart tin, pressing into the edges so that the mixture comes up the sides of the tin slightly. Cover and place in the freezer to firm. Meanwhile, make the ricotta cream as above, then spread over the pie base, cover and return to the freezer for 15 minutes to chill. Scatter with 125 g (4 oz) hulled and sliced strawberries, then serve immediately.

CAK-PIES-DAR

3 Caramel Chocolate Fondants

Serves 6

200 g (7 oz) unsalted butter, plus extra for greasing

225 g (7½ oz) plain dark chocolate, broken into small pieces

50 g (2 oz) plain flour, plus extra for dusting

3 large eggs, plus 2 large egg yolks

75 g (3 oz) soft light brown sugar

6 dessertspoons dulce de leche or thick caramel sauce

ice cream, to serve

- Place the butter and chocolate in a small saucepan over a low heat and warm until just melted. Stir gently, then set aside.

- Meanwhile, grease 6 x 200 ml (7 fl oz) freezer-proof and heatproof ramekins or metal pudding moulds with butter and dust lightly with flour, then place on a baking sheet.

- Place the eggs plus egg yolks and sugar in a large bowl and beat with a hand-held electric whisk until thick and creamy. Fold in the flour and melted chocolate.

- Spoon the mixture into the prepared dishes and dollop 1 spoonful of the dulce de leche or caramel sauce into the centre of each one, then cover with a little of the chocolate mixture. Place in the freezer for 8–10 minutes.

- Remove from the freezer and bake in a preheated oven, 200°C (400°F), Gas Mark 6, for 12–14 minutes until almost firm but still with a slight wobble in the centre. Leave to cool in the dishes for 2 minutes, then invert on to serving dishes and serve each with a scoop of ice cream.

Caramel Chocolate Tarts

Melt 100 g (3½ oz) plain dark chocolate in a heatproof bowl set over a saucepan of gently simmering water. Meanwhile, place 1 tablespoon thick caramel sauce into each of 6 x 8 cm (3½ inch) shop-bought sweet pastry cases. Drizzle over the chocolate and sprinkle over 2 tablespoons toasted chopped hazelnuts. Freeze for 5 minutes until the chocolate has set.

Caramel Chocolate Soufflés

Melt 175 g (6 oz) plain dark chocolate, broken into small pieces, 15 g (½ oz) unsalted butter, 1 tablespoon thick caramel sauce and ½ teaspoon vanilla extract in a heatproof bowl set over a saucepan of gently simmering water. Stir gently, then scrape into a large bowl and set aside. Meanwhile, grease 6 x 175 ml (6 fl oz) ramekins and dust with cocoa powder, then place on a baking sheet. Whisk 3 large egg whites in a clean bowl with a hand-held electric whisk until stiff, then gradually whisk in 75 g (3 oz) caster sugar. Beat 3 large egg yolks into the chocolate mixture, then fold in the egg whites. Spoon into the ramekins and bake in a preheated oven, 200°C (400°F), Gas Mark 6, for 10–12 minutes until risen. Serve immediately.

30 Cherry Cream Horns

Makes 8

butter, for greasing
200 g (7 oz) chilled puff pastry
flour, for dusting
beaten egg, to glaze
3 tablespoons granulated sugar
125 g (4 oz) pitted cherries,
   thawed if frozen
150 ml (¼ pint) double cream
50 g (2 oz) vanilla sugar

- Grease 8 cream horn moulds with butter and line a baking sheet with nonstick baking paper. Roll out the pastry on a floured surface to about 40 x 12 cm (16 x 5 inches) and cut into 8 long strips, then wind 1 strip around a mould, starting at the thin end and overlapping slightly, leaving a gap at the wide end. Place on the prepared baking sheet, cover and chill. Repeat with the remaining pastry strips.

- Brush the pastry with beaten egg and sprinkle over the granulated sugar. Bake in a preheated oven, 200°C (400°F), Gas Mark 6, for 12 minutes, or until puffed and golden. Transfer to a wire rack to cool.

- Meanwhile, reserve 8 of the cherries, then roughly chop the remainder. Whip the cream and vanilla sugar in a bowl with a hand-held electric whisk until fairly thick but not dry, then fold in the chopped cherries.

- Carefully twist the moulds from the cooled pastry, then place 1 reserved cherry in the bottom of each cone. Spoon in the cherry cream and serve immediately.

---

1 Cherry Cream Pie

Whip 150 ml (¼ pint) double cream and 50 g (2 oz) vanilla sugar until it forms soft peaks. Cover the base of a 20 cm (8 inch) shop-bought sweet pastry case with 150 g (5 oz) shop-bought fresh custard. Top with 150 g (5 oz) pitted cherries, then spoon over the cream. Scatter over an extra 75 g (3 oz) pitted cherries and some plain dark chocolate curls.

2 Cherry Cream Slices

Unroll 1 sheet from a 425 g (14 oz) pack ready-rolled puff pastry, thawed if frozen, and cut out 4 rectangles, about 6 x 12 cm (2½ x 5 inches). Place on a baking sheet lined with nonstick baking paper. Prick all over with a fork, brush with beaten egg and dust with vanilla sugar. Bake in a preheated oven, 220°C (425°F), Gas Mark 7, for 8–10 minutes until puffed and golden.

Let cool on a wire rack. Meanwhile, whip 150 ml (¼ pint) double cream and 50 g (2 oz) vanilla sugar until it forms soft peaks, then fold in 75 g (3 oz) shop-bought fresh custard. Split each piece of puff pastry in half and fill with one-quarter of the custard cream. Top the slices with 100 g (3½ oz) fresh pitted cherries, then sandwich together with the pastry tops. Serve dusted with icing sugar.

CAK-PIES-BOS

1 Vanilla and Berry-Soaked Sponge Puddings

Serves 6

1 vanilla pod, split lengthways

400 g (13 oz) frozen forest fruit berries

50 g (2 oz) soft dark brown sugar

1 medium sponge flan base, cut into 6 wedges

6 scoops of vanilla ice cream or clotted cream

- Scrape the seeds from the vanilla pod and place both the seeds and pod in a saucepan with the berries and sugar. Heat gently, stirring occasionally, until the sugar has dissolved and the fruit collapsed.

- Arrange the sponge wedges in 6 serving dishes and spoon over the warm berries, discarding the vanilla pod. Top each portion with 1 scoop of vanilla ice cream or clotted cream and serve immediately.

2 Berry Sorbet with Vanilla Fingers

Place 250 g (8 oz) frozen mixed fruits, 50 g (2 oz) icing sugar, the seeds scraped from 1 vanilla pod, the finely grated rind of 1 orange and 75 ml (3 fl oz) cranberry juice in a food processor and blend until thick and smooth. Scrape into a shallow container and place in the freezer for 15–18 minutes. Meanwhile, place 2 large egg yolks and 50 g (2 oz) caster sugar in a bowl and beat with a hand-held electric whisk until pale and thick and the whisk leaves a trail when lifted above the mixture. Whisk 2 large egg whites in a clean bowl with a hand-held electric whisk until they form soft peaks, then gradually whisk in 25 g (1 oz) vanilla sugar and a pinch of salt. Fold the whites gently into the yolk mixture, then spoon into

a piping bag fitted with a 1 cm (½ inch) plain nozzle and pipe out about 12 x 8 cm (3½ inch) lengths, well spaced apart, on 2 baking sheets lined with nonstick baking paper. Bake in a preheated oven, 200°C (400°F), Gas Mark 6, for 8–10 minutes until pale golden. Transfer to a wire rack to cool slightly. Scoop the frozen sorbet into 6 serving dishes and serve with the vanilla sponge fingers.

3 Vanilla Berry Sponge Pudding

Mix together 400 g (13 oz) frozen forest fruit berries and 50 g (2 oz) soft dark brown sugar in a bowl, then tip evenly into a greased medium ovenproof dish. Drizzle over 3 tablespoons maple syrup. Place 125 g (4 oz) softened unsalted butter, 125 g (4 oz) golden caster sugar, 2 large lightly beaten eggs, 1 teaspoon vanilla bean paste or extract, 125 g (4 oz) sifted self-raising flour and 1 teaspoon baking powder in a bowl and beat together with a hand-held electric whisk until combined, then spoon evenly over the fruit. Bake in a preheated oven, 200°C (400°F), Gas Mark 6, for 20–25 minutes until risen and golden. Serve warm with ice cream or clotted cream and warm ready-made red fruit coulis.

30 Pistachio and Chocolate Danish Pastries

Serves 4

375 g (12 oz) chilled ready-rolled
   puff pastry
50 g (2 oz) shop-bought thick,
   fresh crème pâtissière or vanilla
   custard
beaten egg, for brushing
50 g (2 oz) plain dark chocolate
   chunks or chips
50 g (2 oz) pistachio nut kernels
4 teaspoons granulated sugar
2 tablespoons icing sugar
1–2 teaspoons milk

- Line a large baking sheet with nonstick baking paper. Unroll the pastry and cut in half widthways to make 2 rectangles. Place each pastry sheet so that the short edge is facing you, then lightly score the surface lengthways into equal thirds.

- Spread the custard evenly over the middle third. Cut the outer thirds of pastry into diagonally slanted strips about 1.5 cm (¾ inch) thick, then brush with beaten egg. Scatter the chocolate chips and two-thirds of the pistachios over the custard, then bring the pastry strips over the filling, alternating the sides to create a plaited effect.

- Roughly chop the remaining pistachios. Brush the pastries with beaten egg, then sprinkle with the chopped pistachios and granulated sugar. Place on the prepared baking sheet and bake in a preheated oven, 200°C (400°F), Gas Mark 6, for 18–20 minutes until golden and puffed.

- Meanwhile, mix the icing sugar with just enough milk to create an icing of drizzling consistency. Remove the pastries from the oven, drizzle over the icing and transfer to wire racks. Cut each pastry in half and serve warm or cold.

 Pistachio and Chocolate Tarts

Toast 100 g (3½ oz) pistachio nut kernels in a preheated oven, 220°C (425°F), Gas Mark 7, for 3–4 minutes. Whip 100 ml (3½ fl oz) double cream and 1 teaspoon grated orange rind until it forms soft peaks. Fold in 50 g (2 oz) cooled, melted plain dark chocolate until just marbled. Spoon into 4 x 8 cm (3½ inch) shop-bought sweet pastry cases and sprinkle with the nuts.

Sticky Pistachio Parcels

Gently melt 25 g (1 oz) butter, 1 teaspoon lemon juice and 3 tablespoons maple syrup in a saucepan, then stir in 25 g (1 oz) fresh white breadcrumbs, 50 g (2 oz) pistachio nut kernels, roughly chopped, and a pinch of ground cinnamon. Brush 4 sheets of filo pastry, about 30 x 40 cm (12 x 16 inches), with 50 g (2 oz) melted butter. Spoon one-quarter of the filling on to one end of each sheet and roll up, tucking in the sides. Brush with more butter, place on a baking sheet lined with nonstick baking paper and bake in a preheated oven, 200°C (400°F), Gas Mark 6, for 10 minutes, until crisp and golden. Serve warm, drizzled with extra maple syrup.

CAK-PIES-NES

 # Cookie Dough Fruit Crumbles

Serves 4

2 ripe but firm pears, peeled, cored and diced, or 400 g (13 oz) can pear halves in juice, drained and diced

125 g (4 oz) raspberries, thawed if frozen

1–2 tablespoons soft dark brown sugar, according to taste

75 g (3 oz) plain flour

50 g (2 oz) cold unsalted butter, diced

100 g (3½ oz) shop-bought chilled cookie dough, chopped cookie dough ice cream, to serve (optional)

- Gently mix together the pears, raspberries and sugar in a bowl, then spoon into 4 large ramekins or a medium ovenproof dish and place on a baking sheet.

- Place the flour and butter in a mini food processor and pulse until the mixture resembles fine breadcrumbs. Add the chopped cookie dough and pulse briefly to mix, but not chop too finely.

- Sprinkle the topping over the fruit and bake in a preheated oven, 220°C (425°F), Gas Mark 7, for 15 minutes, or until golden. Serve with scoops of cookie dough ice cream, if liked.

 ### Cookie Dough Cheesecakes

Place 175 g (6 oz) chocolate chip cookies in a freezer bag and tap lightly with a rolling pin until crushed. Tip into a bowl and mix with 50 g (2 oz) melted unsalted butter until well coated. Press the biscuits into 4 x 12 cm (5 inch) lightly greased, loose-bottomed tart tins, then cover and place in the freezer to chill. Meanwhile, place 250 g (8 oz) cream cheese, 100 ml (3½ fl oz) double cream and 1 teaspoon vanilla bean paste or the seeds scraped from 1 vanilla pod in a large bowl and beat together with a hand-held electric whisk until thick and smooth. Fold in 150 g (5 oz) chocolate chip cookies, broken into pieces, then spoon on to the chilled biscuit bases. Push the cheesecakes out of their tins and serve immediately with 100 g (3 oz) blueberries.

Cookie Dough Crumble Tart

Unroll 375 g (12 oz) chilled ready-rolled puff pastry and place on a baking sheet lined with nonstick baking paper, then score a 1.5 cm (¾ inch) border around the edge. Brush with 25 g (1 oz) melted unsalted butter, then sprinkle 25 g (1 oz) ground almonds inside the border. Top with 2 peeled, cored and sliced pears, 125 g (4 oz) raspberries and 175 g (6 oz) crumbled shop-bought chilled cookie dough. Bake in a preheated oven, 200°C (400°F), Gas Mark 6, for 18–20 minutes until crisp and golden. Serve with cookie dough ice-cream, if liked.

3 Caramelized Pear Tarte Tatin

Serves 4-6

50 g (2 oz) unsalted butter
75g (3 oz) soft dark brown sugar
4–5 ripe but firm pears, peeled,
  cored and sliced into eighths, or
  2 x 410 g (13 oz) cans pear
  halves in juice, drained
250 g (8 oz) shop-bought chilled
  shortcrust pastry
crème fraîche, to serve

- Place the butter and sugar in a 25 cm (10 inch) nonstick, ovenproof frying pan and heat gently until melted. Add the pears and cook gently for 5–6 minutes, turning occasionally, until lightly caramelized, then arrange neatly in the pan.

- Meanwhile, roll out the pastry on a floured surface and cut out a circle about 1 cm (½ inch) larger than the pan. Lay the pastry over the pan, carefully tucking it in around the edges to completely cover the pears. Prick with a fork and bake in a preheated oven, 220°C (425°F), Gas Mark 7, for 15–18 minutes until crisp and golden.

- Leave to cool in the pan for 1–2 minutes, then carefully invert on to a large serving plate and cut into wedges. Serve with crème fraîche.

---

1 **Tarte Tatin Pear Cheesecakes**

Divide 4 dessertspoons good-quality ready-made toffee sauce between 4 x 200 ml (7 fl oz) ramekins. Peel, core and slice 2 ripe pears, or use a drained 400 g (13 oz) can pear halves in juice, and arrange the slices over the toffee sauce. Place 200 g (7 oz) cream cheese, 100 g (3½ oz) mascarpone cheese, 50 g (2 oz) soft light brown sugar and 1 teaspoon grated lemon rind in a bowl and beat together with a hand-held electric whisk until thick and smooth. Spoon the mixture into the ramekins and spread thickly to cover the pears. Place 150 g (5 oz) shortbread biscuits in a freezer bag and tap lightly with a rolling pin until crushed. Tip into a bowl and mix with 3 tablespoons melted unsalted butter until well coated. Divide between the ramekins, flattening gently. Serve immediately or chill until required.

2 **Cheat's Pear Tarte Tatin**

Unroll 325 g (11 oz) ready-rolled puff pastry and cut out 4 x 12 cm (5 inch) rounds. Place on a baking sheet lined with nonstick baking paper, brush with melted butter and prick with a fork. Bake in a preheated oven, 220°C (425°F), Gas Mark 7, for 12–15 minutes until puffed and golden. Meanwhile, melt 50 g (2 oz) butter and 75 g (3 oz) soft dark brown sugar in a large frying pan, then add 4 peeled, cored and quartered pears and cook gently for 10 minutes, or until caramelized. Dust the pastry with icing sugar, spoon over the pears and serve with crème fraîche.

20 Pear Samosas with Ginger Sauce

Serves 4

2 ripe but firm pears, peeled,
   cored and diced
50 g (2 oz) walnuts, roughly
   chopped
50 g (2 oz) soft dark brown sugar
1 teaspoon ground ginger
15 g (½ oz) piece of stem ginger
   in syrup, cut into matchsticks
4 sheets of filo pastry, about
   30 x 40 cm (12 x 16 inches)
25 g (1 oz) unsalted butter, melted

For the ginger sauce

50 g (2 oz) unsalted butter
50 ml (2 fl oz) double cream
25 g (1 oz) soft dark brown sugar
½ teaspoon ground ginger
15 g (½ oz) piece of stem ginger
   in syrup, cut into matchsticks
2 tablespoons stem ginger syrup
   (taken from the jar)

- To make the ginger sauce, place all the ingredients in a small saucepan and heat gently, stirring occasionally, until the mixture is smooth. Set aside.

- Meanwhile, line a large baking sheet with nonstick baking paper. Place the pears, walnuts, brown sugar, ground ginger and stem ginger in a bowl and mix to combine.

- Lay the filo sheets on a clean surface and brush each with a little melted butter. Divide the pear mixture between the sheets, then fold up into triangles to resemble samosas.

- Place on the prepared baking sheet, brush with any remaining butter and bake in a preheated oven, 220°C (425°F), Gas Mark 7, for 8–10 minutes until golden and crisp. Serve warm with the ginger sauce.

10 Ginger Snaps with Fruit Compote

Place 500 g (1 lb) rhubarb, cut into 2 cm (¾ inch) chunks, in a saucepan with 125 g (4 oz) soft light brown sugar, 1 teaspoon ground ginger and 50 ml (2 fl oz) orange juice. Heat gently until the sugar has dissolved, then bring to the boil and simmer for 6 minutes. Add 3 peeled and quartered pears and cook for 3 minutes more. Serve each portion of compote with 2 ginger brandy snaps.

30 Pear and Ginger Strudel

Mix together a drained 400 g (13 oz) can pear halves, chopped, ½ teaspoon each of ground ginger and cinnamon, 50 g (2 oz) sultanas, 1 teaspoon finely grated lemon rind, 25 g (1 oz) demerara sugar and 25 g (1 oz) chopped toasted hazelnuts in a large bowl. Brush 3 sheets of filo pastry, about 30 x 40 cm (12 x 16 inches), with melted unsalted butter and lay on top of each other on a baking sheet lined with nonstick baking paper. Sprinkle with 25 g (1 oz) fresh white breadcrumbs and top with the fruit, leaving a 5 mm (¼ inch) border around the edge. Tuck in the edges and roll up lengthways. Bake in a preheated oven, 220°C (425°F), Gas Mark 7, for 18–20 minutes until the strudel is crisp and golden. Dust with ½ teaspoon ground ginger and 1 tablespoon icing sugar and serve cut into slices.

30 White Chocolate and Raspberry Baskets

Serves 8

175 g (6 oz) white chocolate
200 g (7 oz) raspberries, plus
   extra to decorate
25 g (1 oz) icing sugar, sifted
350 ml (12 fl oz) double cream
white chocolate curls, to decorate

Brandy snap baskets

50 g (2 oz) golden caster sugar
2 tablespoons golden syrup
½ tablespoon brandy
50 g (2 oz) unsalted butter, plus
   extra for greasing
50 g (2 oz) plain flour
½ teaspoon ground ginger

- Line 2 large baking sheets with nonstick baking paper. Place the sugar, golden syrup, brandy and butter in a small saucepan and cook over a low heat, stirring occasionally, until the sugar has dissolved. Sift in the flour and ginger and stir until smooth.

- Drop 8 heaped tablespoonfuls of the mixture, well spaced apart, on to the baking sheets and bake in a preheated oven, 200°C (400°F), Gas Mark 6, for 5–7 minutes until lacy and golden. Meanwhile, turn 8 small bowls upside-down and lightly grease with butter.

- Let the brandy snaps cool slightly, then quickly lift off using a palette knife and place on the upturned bowls, moulding to their shape. Leave to harden.

- Meanwhile, melt the chocolate in a heatproof bowl set over a saucepan of gently simmering water, then leave to cool. Place the raspberries and icing sugar in a bowl and lightly crush together.

- Whip the cream in a large bowl until it forms soft peaks, then fold in the cooled chocolate. Fold in the crushed raspberries until just combined.

- Place the cooled baskets on serving plates, spoon in the raspberry cream and decorate with extra raspberries and white chocolate curls. Serve immediately.

---

1 **Red Fruit Fools with Brandy Snaps**

Fold 250 g (8 oz) red fruit yogurt and 150 g (5 oz) melted, cooled white chocolate into 200 ml (7 fl oz) whipped double cream. Spoon into 8 dishes and drizzle 1 tablespoon ready-made red fruit coulis over each. Decorate with 8 brandy snaps, broken into shards.

2 **Brandy Snaps with Raspberry Cream**

Make the brandy snaps as above, but cool the biscuits on a wooden rolling pin. Meanwhile, melt 150 g (5 oz) white chocolate in a heatproof bowl set over a saucepan of gently simmering water, then leave to cool. Whip 300 ml (½ pint) double cream in a large bowl until it forms soft peaks, then fold in the cooled chocolate. Place 150 g (5 oz) raspberries and 25 g (1 oz) icing sugar in a blender and blend until smooth. Swirl into the cream, then spoon into 8 small serving dishes. Grate over extra white chocolate and serve with the brandy snaps.

CAK-PIES-HOK

Macadamia and Apple Crunch

Serves 6

25 g (1 oz) unsalted butter, melted
25 g (1 oz) demerara sugar
4 dessert apples, such as Cox,
   peeled, cored and roughly
   chopped
1 tablespoon lemon juice
clotted cream, to serve

Crunchy topping

75 g (3 oz) rolled oats
50 g (2 oz) macadamia nuts,
   chopped
50 g (2 oz) demerara sugar
50 g (2 oz) unsalted butter,
   melted

- Line a baking sheet with nonstick baking paper. To make the crunchy topping, put all the ingredients in a bowl and stir until well coated, then tip on to the baking sheet. Bake in a preheated oven, 200°C (400°F), Gas Mark 6, for 5–7 minutes, stirring occasionally to prevent burning, until golden and crispy. Tip into a bowl and leave to cool slightly.

- Meanwhile, place the melted butter and demerara sugar in a nonstick frying pan and heat gently until melted, then add the apples and lemon juice and cook over a medium heat for 2–3 minutes, stirring occasionally, until the apples are softened but still holding their shape.

- Spoon the apples into 6 serving dishes and sprinkle over the topping. Serve with clotted cream.

---

2 Crunchy Nut Apple Custard

Place 25 g (1 oz) unsalted butter and 25 g (1 oz) demerara sugar in a nonstick frying pan and heat gently until melted, then add 4 dessert apples, peeled, cored and roughly chopped, and 1 tablespoon lemon juice and cook over a medium heat for 2–3 minutes, stirring occasionally, until the apples are softened and golden but still holding their shape. Mix together 1 teaspoon mixed spice and 300 ml (½ pint) shop-bought fresh custard in a jug, then pour into a medium ovenproof dish and scatter over the apples. Mix together the crunchy topping ingredients as above, then tip over the apples. Bake in a preheated oven, 200°C (400°F), Gas Mark 6, for 15 minutes, or until heated through and golden. Serve warm with clotted cream or ice cream.

3 Crunchy Nut and Apple Pies

Roll out 200 g (7 oz) chilled sweet pastry, cut out 6 x 10 cm (4 inch) rounds and use to line 6 greased tartlet tins. Place on a baking sheet. Mix together 3 coarsely grated apples, 1 teaspoon mixed spice, 2 tablespoons soft light brown sugar and 1 tablespoon lemon juice, then divide between the cases. Mix together the crunchy topping ingredients as above, then spoon over the apples. Bake in a preheated oven, 200°C (400°F), Gas Mark 6, for 18–20 minutes until golden. Serve warm with clotted cream.

Fruity Ginger Sponge Gratin

Serves 6–8

250 g (8 oz) Greek yogurt
125 g (4 oz) mascarpone cheese
½ teaspoon ground ginger
1 shop-bought Jamaica ginger
  loaf cake, sliced
500 g (1 lb) mixed fruit, such as
  papaya, kiwi, mango and
  strawberries, roughly chopped
50 g (2 oz) soft dark brown sugar

For the ginger syrup

2 x 15 g (½ oz) pieces of stem
  ginger in syrup, chopped
1 tablespoon stem ginger syrup
  (taken from the jar)
1 teaspoon finely grated lemon rind
25 g (1 oz) unsalted butter
1 tablespoon runny honey

- First, make the ginger syrup. Place all the ingredients in a small saucepan over a low heat and warm until just melted. Stir gently, then set aside.

- Meanwhile, beat together the yogurt, mascarpone and ground ginger in a large bowl until smooth. Arrange the cake slices in a shallow ovenproof dish.

- Place the mixed fruit in a large bowl, then pour over the syrup and mix gently to coat. Tip the fruit over the cake, then spoon over the yogurt mixture and sprinkle with the brown sugar.

- Slide under a preheated hot grill for about 3 minutes, or until the sugar has melted. Serve immediately.

Ginger Sponge with Mango Coulis

Place 250 g (8 oz) chopped mango, 2 x 15 g (½ oz) pieces of stem ginger in syrup, chopped, 1 tablespoon stem ginger syrup (taken from the jar), 1 teaspoon finely grated lemon rind and 2 teaspoons lemon juice in a small saucepan over a low heat and warm until the fruit is just softened. Transfer to a food processor and blend until smooth. Leave to cool slightly. Meanwhile, cut 1 shop-bought Jamaica ginger loaf cake into 6 slices. Whisk together 1 large egg and 250 ml (8 fl oz) milk in a bowl and place 75 g (3 oz) demerara sugar on a plate. Dip both sides of the ginger cake slices into the eggy mixture, then dip into the sugar until well coated. Heat 50 g (2 oz) butter in a nonstick frying pan, add the cake slices and cook for 1–2 minutes on each side until golden and crisp. Dust with icing sugar and serve with the mango coulis.

Stem Ginger Sponge Puddings

Spoon 1 tablespoon golden syrup into each of 6 greased 175 ml (6 fl oz) metal pudding moulds. Beat together 2 large eggs, 1 teaspoon ground ginger, 2 x 15 g (½ oz) pieces of stem ginger in syrup, chopped, and 100 g (3½ oz) each of golden caster sugar, softened unsalted butter and self-raising flour until combined, then spoon into the moulds. Bake in a preheated oven, 200°C (400°F), Gas Mark 6, for 20 minutes or until risen and golden. Turn out and serve with custard.

Banana and Caramel Sponge Tart

Serves 4–6

6 tablespoons dulce de leche or thick caramel sauce

1 medium sponge flan base

2 bananas, thickly sliced

150 ml (¼ pint) whipping or double cream

plain dark chocolate curls, to decorate

- Spread the dulce de leche or caramel sauce thickly over the sponge base, then arrange the sliced bananas on top.

- Whip the cream in a bowl with a hand-held electric whisk until it forms soft peaks, then spoon over the bananas. Top with chocolate curls and serve in wedges.

 Banana Fudge Cakes

Place 100 g (3½ oz) softened unsalted butter, 100 g (3½ oz) soft dark brown sugar, 1 large lightly beaten egg, 100 g (3½ oz) self-raising flour, ½ teaspoon baking powder and 1 mashed banana in a bowl and beat together with a hand-held electric whisk until combined. Place 25 g (1 oz) sweetened dried banana chips in a freezer bag and tap lightly with a rolling pin until broken up, then fold into the mixture with 75 g (3 oz) baking fudge chunks. Spoon into a greased or paper case-lined 12-hole nonstick cupcake or muffin tin. Bake in a preheated oven, 200°C (400°F), Gas Mark 6, for 12–14 minutes until risen and golden. Transfer to a wire rack to cool slightly. Serve warm drizzled with warmed dulce de leche, if liked.

 Upside-Down Banana and Caramel Cakes Arrange

2 small, sliced bananas over the base of 6 well-greased 175 ml (6 fl oz) metal pudding moulds. Drop 1 dessertspoon dulce de leche or thick caramel sauce into each one. Place 100 g (3½ oz) softened unsalted butter, 75 g (3 oz) soft light brown sugar, 1 large lightly beaten egg and 1 mashed, ripe banana in a large bowl and beat together with a hand-held electric whisk until combined. Sift in 100 g (3½ oz) self-raising flour and ½ teaspoon baking powder, then fold in. Spoon the mixture into the moulds and bake in a preheated oven, 200°C (400°F), Gas Mark 6, for 18–20 minutes until risen and golden. Invert the cakes on to 6 serving dishes and serve warm with custard or single cream.

CAK-PIES-CUB

Crunchy Peach and Strawberry Cranachan

Serves 4-6

75 g (3 oz) rolled oats

50 g (2 oz) demerara sugar

50 g (2 oz) chopped hazelnuts or mixed chopped nuts

350 ml (12 fl oz) double cream

2 tablespoons runny honey

100 g (3½ oz) mascarpone cheese

2 tablespoons peach liqueur (optional)

150 g (5 oz) strawberries, hulled and diced

400 g (13 oz) can peach slices in juice

- Line a baking sheet with nonstick baking paper. Mix together the oats, sugar and nuts in a bowl, then sprinkle evenly over the baking sheet. Bake in a preheated oven, 200°C (400°F), Gas Mark 6, for 6–7 minutes, stirring occasionally, until lightly toasted and golden. Tip into a bowl and leave to cool.

- Meanwhile, whip the cream, honey, mascarpone and peach liqueur, if using, in a bowl with a hand-held electric whisk until thick and creamy. Fold in most of the strawberries, reserving a few for decoration.

- Divide the peaches between 4–6 serving glasses, alternating with layers of the cream mixture and the crunchy oats. Serve immediately, decorated with the reserved strawberries.

---

1 Peachy Granola Crunch

Tip 150 g (5 oz) granola-style muesli on to a baking sheet and place in a preheated oven, 200°C (400°F), Gas Mark 6, for 5–6 minutes, stirring occasionally, until golden. Tip into a bowl and leave to cool. Meanwhile, slice 4 stoned peaches and arrange in the bottom of a large glass bowl. Hull and roughly chop 200 g (7 oz) strawberries and mix into 250 g (8 oz) Greek yogurt with 1 tablespoon maple syrup. Spoon over the peaches and sprinkle over the toasted muesli. Serve drizzled with extra maple syrup, if liked.

3 Golden Oaty Peaches

Arrange 4 stoned and halved peaches in an ovenproof dish, cut side up. Place 50 g (2 oz) plain flour, 1 teaspoon ground cinnamon, a pinch of salt and 75 g (3 oz) cold, diced unsalted butter in a food processor and pulse until the mixture resembles fine breadcrumbs. Add 50 g (2 oz) demerara sugar, 50 g (2 oz) rolled oats and 50 g (2 oz) chopped pecan nuts and pulse briefly to combine. Drizzle 2 tablespoons peach liqueur over the peaches and top with the crumble mixture. Bake in a preheated oven, 200°C (400°F),

Gas Mark 6, for 18–20 minutes until the peaches are softened and the topping golden. Serve with sliced strawberries, if liked, and dollops of crème fraîche.

10 Blackberry Fools with Almond Tuiles

Serves 6

100 g (3½ oz) frozen blackberries
50 g (2 oz) icing sugar
200 ml (7 fl oz) double cream
300 g (10 oz) Greek yogurt

To serve

fresh blackberries (optional)
12 shop-bought almond tuiles

- Place the frozen blackberries and icing sugar in a blender or food processor and blend until smooth.

- Whip the cream in a bowl with a hand-held electric whisk until it forms soft peaks. Fold in the yogurt and blackberry purée and spoon into 6 serving glasses.

- Scatter with fresh blackberries, if using, and serve immediately with the almond tuiles.

20 Blackberry Almond Tartlets

Place 1 large egg, 50 g (2 oz) ground almonds, 50 g (2 oz) softened unsalted butter, 50 g (2 oz) caster sugar and ½ teaspoon vanilla extract in a bowl and beat together with a hand-held electric whisk until smooth, then spoon into 6 x 8 cm (3½ inch) shop-bought sweet pastry cases on a baking sheet. Dot with about 50 g (2 oz) fresh blackberries and bake in a preheated oven, 200°C (400°F), Gas Mark 6, for 15 minutes, or until golden. Serve warm or cold, dusted with icing sugar.

30 Blackberry Bakewell Tart

Unroll a 225 g (7 oz) ready-rolled shortcrust pastry round, thawed if frozen, and use to line a greased 23 cm (9 inch) fluted tart tin, trimming away any excess. Spread 75 g (3 oz) blackberry jam over the base. Place 75 g (3 oz) softened unsalted butter, 75 g (3 oz) ground almonds, 75 g (3 oz) caster sugar, 1 large egg plus 1 large egg yolk, 25 g (1 oz) plain flour and 2 teaspoons milk in a bowl and beat together with a hand-held electric whisk until smooth, then spoon evenly over the jam. Scatter over 25 g (1 oz) flaked almonds and bake in a preheated oven, 200°C (400°F), Gas Mark 6, for 20–22 minutes until golden and just firm to the touch. Serve warm or cold in wedges, dusted with icing sugar.

30 Cherry Almond Tart

Serves 6–8

4 sheets of filo pastry, about
   30 x 40 cm (12 x 16 inches)
50 g (2 oz) unsalted butter,
   melted
2 large eggs
75 g (3 oz) ground almonds
25 g (1 oz) chopped almonds
100 g (3½ oz) caster sugar
1 teaspoon almond or vanilla
   extract
150 g (5 oz) pitted cherries,
   thawed if frozen
25 g (1 oz) whole blanched
   almonds
icing sugar, for dusting (optional)

- Lay the filo sheets on a clean surface and brush each with the melted butter, then arrange in a lightly greased 23 cm (9 inch) tart or cake tin so that the edges overlap the side of the tin.

- Place the eggs, ground almonds, chopped almonds, sugar and almond or vanilla extract in a bowl and beat together with a hand-held electric whisk until combined. Spread the mixture evenly over the filo base, then scatter with the cherries and whole almonds. Scrunch in the edges of the pastry without covering the top.

- Drizzle the remaining butter over the pastry and bake in a preheated oven, 220°C (425°F), Gas Mark 7, for 18–20 minutes until golden and firm to the touch. Leave to cool in the tin for 2–3 minutes, then turn out and serve dusted with icing sugar, if liked.

10 Cherry Almond Trifles

Arrange 3 thickly sliced almond croissants in 6 tumblers. Drain 2 x 425 g (14 oz) can pitted black cherries in syrup, reserving the syrup. Divide half the cherries between the glasses and drizzle 1 tablespoon of the syrup over each one. Blend the remaining cherries in a food processor until almost smooth. Beat together 300 g (10 oz) mascarpone, 3 tablespoons icing sugar and 2 teaspoons finely grated orange rind then fold in the blended cherries and spoon into the tumblers. Decorate with whipped cream and toasted almonds.

20 Cherry and Almond Cobbler

Place 50 g (2 oz) unsalted butter and 50 g (2 oz) soft light brown sugar in a frying pan and heat gently until melted, then add 4 peeled, cored and thickly sliced dessert apples and cook gently for 6–7 minutes until slightly softened and golden. Stir in 150 g (5 oz) pitted cherries, thawed if frozen, 1 teaspoon almond or vanilla extract and 25 g (1 oz) chopped almonds and warm through, then scrape into a medium ovenproof dish. Slice 3 shop-bought fruit scones in half and arrange, cut side down, over the fruit. Drizzle with 25 g (1 oz) melted unsalted butter and scatter over 25 g (1 oz) flaked almonds. Bake in a preheated oven, 200°C (400°F), Gas Mark 6, for 8–10 minutes until hot and bubbling and the almonds are golden. Serve warm with custard, if liked.

CAK-PIES-LUO

Chocolate Stracciatella Brownie Cheesecakes

Serves 6

4 fudge-textured brownies, cubed

250 g (8 oz) cream cheese

100 g (3½ oz) fromage frais

75 g (3 oz) golden caster sugar

75 g (3 oz) milk chocolate, finely chopped or coarsely grated

milk or plain dark chocolate curls, to decorate

- Divide the chocolate brownie cubes between 6 glass ramekins or bowls and press down lightly.

- Place the cream cheese, fromage frais and sugar in a large bowl and beat together with a hand-held electric whisk until thick and smooth. Add the chocolate and beat to combine, then spoon over the brownie bases.

- Scatter over the chocolate curls and serve immediately or chill until required.

 Stracciatella Choc Cheesecake

Place 200 g (7 oz) chocolate cookies in a freezer bag and tap lightly with a rolling pin until crushed. Tip into a bowl and mix with 50 g (2 oz) melted unsalted butter until well coated. Press into a 23 cm (9 inch) fluted tart tin and chill, covered, in the freezer. Meanwhile, melt 50 g (2 oz) plain dark or milk chocolate, broken into small pieces, in a heatproof bowl set over a saucepan of gently simmering water, ensuring the bowl does not touch the water, then leave to cool. Place 250 g (8 oz) cream cheese, 100 g (3½ oz) fromage frais and 75 g (3 oz) golden caster sugar in a large bowl and beat together with a hand-held electric whisk until thick and smooth. Add 75 g

 (3 oz) milk chocolate, finely chopped or coarsely grated, and beat to combine. Spoon the mixture into the chilled tart, then drizzle over the cooled chocolate and swirl the surface with a fork. Return the cake to the freezer for about 10 minutes, or until the chocolate has set. Serve in wedges, sprinkled with white chocolate curls or grated white chocolate.

Gooey Chocolate Pudding

Pour 75 g (3 oz) melted and cooled unsalted butter, 100 ml (3½ fl oz) milk and 1 large egg into a bowl and whisk until smooth. Sift in 125 g (4 oz) self-raising flour and 2 tablespoons good-quality cocoa powder, add 75 g (3 oz) soft light brown sugar and beat to combine. Fold in 75 g (3 oz) chocolate chips. Pour the mixture into a medium ovenproof dish. Mix together 50 g (2 oz) soft light brown sugar, 1 tablespoon cocoa powder and 125 ml (4 fl oz) boiling water in a heatproof bowl, then pour over the top of the sponge. Bake in a preheated oven, 200°C (400°F), Gas Mark 6, for 18–20 minutes until just firm to the touch. Serve with single cream.

30 Sticky Pecan Pie

Serves 6

25 g (1 oz) unsalted butter, plus extra for greasing
150 g (5 oz) golden syrup
1 tablespoon lemon juice
1 teaspoon finely grated lemon rind
50 g (2 oz) soft light brown sugar
200 g (7 oz) pecan halves
225 g (7 oz) ready-rolled shortcrust pastry round, thawed if frozen
2 large eggs
vanilla ice cream, to serve

- Lightly grease a 23 cm (9 inch) pie dish. Place the butter and golden syrup in a small saucepan over a low heat and warm until just melted. Pour into a bowl and stir in the lemon juice and rind, sugar and pecan halves. Leave to cool for 1–2 minutes.

- Meanwhile, unroll the pastry and use to line the prepared pie dish, trimming away the excess pastry. Beat the eggs into the cooled butter mixture, then pour into the pastry case.

- Bake in a preheated oven, 200°C (400°F), Gas Mark 6, for 20 minutes, or until golden and just set. Leave to cool in the dish for 5 minutes, then cut into slices and serve warm with scoops of vanilla ice cream.

---

10 Sticky Pecan Pudding

Place 15 g (½ oz) unsalted butter and 75 g (3 oz) golden syrup in a small saucepan over a low heat and warm until just melted, then stir in 1½ teaspoons lemon juice, ½ teaspoon grated lemon rind and 100 g (3½ oz) pecan halves. Meanwhile, cut a 300 g (10 oz) shop-bought golden syrup cake into slices and arrange in an ovenproof dish so that the slices are just overlapping. Spoon over the sauce and bake in a preheated oven, 220°C (425°F), Gas Mark 7, for 5–6 minutes until hot and bubbling. Leave to cool slightly, then serve warm with vanilla ice cream.

20 Sticky Pecan Parcels

Place 25 g (1 oz) unsalted butter and 100 g (3½ oz) golden syrup in a small saucepan over a low heat and warm until just melted. Stir in 1 teaspoon lemon juice, ½ teaspoon finely grated lemon rind, 25 g (1 oz) soft light brown sugar, 100 g (3½ oz) chopped pecan halves and 25 g (1 oz) fresh white breadcrumbs. Brush 6 sheets of filo pastry, about 30 x 40 cm (12 x 16 inches), with melted unsalted butter, then fold each sheet in half. Brush with more butter and divide the pecan filling between the sheets. Roll up like parcels, tucking in the sides, then lay on 2 baking sheets lined with nonstick baking paper and brush with more melted butter. Bake in a preheated oven, 200°C (400°F), Gas Mark 6, for 10 minutes, or until crisp and golden. Leave to cool slightly, then serve warm with vanilla ice cream.

Crunchy Chocolate Pears

Serves 4

150 g (5 oz) shop-bought Belgian chocolate sauce

4 ripe, but firm pears, peeled, cored and halved

4 scoops of good-quality chocolate ice cream

75 g (3 oz) chocolate chip shortbread cookies, crumbled

- Gently warm through the chocolate sauce in a saucepan.

- Meanwhile, divide the pear halves between 4 serving dishes, then top each portion with 1 scoop of the ice cream.

- Pour over the warmed chocolate sauce and top with the crumbled biscuits. Serve immediately.

 Pear and Chocolate Turnovers Unroll 375 g (12 oz) chilled ready-rolled puff pastry on a floured surface and cut into 4 x 15 cm (6 inch) squares. Spread 1½ tablespoons chocolate hazelnut spread over the centre of each square and top each with a drained canned pear half. Bring 2 opposite corners of the pastry up and over the pear, and squeeze together, then brush with beaten egg and place on a baking sheet lined with nonstick baking paper. Sprinkle 1 teaspoon granulated sugar over each turnover and bake in a preheated oven, 230°C (450°F) Gas Mark 8, for 12–14 minutes until puffed, golden and crisp. Serve warm with double cream and grated plain dark chocolate.

 Rich Pear and Chocolate Pie Unroll 375 g (12 oz) chilled ready-rolled puff pastry and place on a baking sheet lined with nonstick baking paper, then score a 1.5 cm (¾ inch) border around the edge. Brush with beaten egg and prick with a fork. Bake in a preheated oven, 200°C (400°F), Gas Mark 6, for 18–20 minutes until puffed and golden. Leave to cool. Meanwhile, heat 125 ml (4 fl oz) double cream in a small saucepan until almost boiling. then pour over 200 g (7 oz) finely chopped or coarsely grated plain dark chocolate in a heatproof bowl and stir until melted. Leave to cool, then beat in 125 g (4 oz) mascarpone cheese. Spread thickly over the cooled puff pastry and arrange 3 peeled, cored and sliced pears over the top. Scatter over 25 g (1 oz) toasted chopped hazelnuts and serve in slices with single cream.

2 **Lemon Meringue Fools**

Serves 4

175 ml (6 fl oz) double cream
150 g (5 oz) mascarpone cheese
25 g (1 oz) icing sugar
½ teaspoon lemon extract
150 g (5 oz) natural yogurt
75 g (3 oz) lemon curd, plus
    4 heaped teaspoons
4 meringue nests, broken into
    small pieces

- Whip the cream, mascarpone, icing sugar and lemon extract in a large bowl with a hand-held electric whisk until it forms soft peaks. Fold in the yogurt and the 75 g (3 oz) lemon curd.

- Spoon the remaining 4 teaspoons lemon curd into 4 tall serving glasses, then spoon in the lemon fool. Chill for 10 minutes.

- Scatter the broken meringues over the fools and serve immediately.

 Mini Lemon Meringues

Place 4 meringue nests on serving plates. Whip 100 ml (3½ fl oz) whipping cream in a bowl with a hand-held electric whisk until it forms soft peaks. Spoon 1 dessertspoon lemon curd into each meringue nest, then dollop over the whipped cream. Scatter 1 teaspoon toasted chopped hazelnuts over each, if liked, then serve immediately.

 Lemon Meringue Pie

Unroll a 225 g (7 oz) ready-rolled shortcrust pastry round, thawed if frozen, and use to line a greased 20 cm (8 inch) fluted tart tin, then line with nonstick baking paper and fill with baking beans. Place in a preheated oven, 220°C (425°F), Gas Mark 7, for 8 minutes, then carefully remove the beans and paper and return the pastry case to the oven for 3–4 minutes until pale golden. Remove from the oven and reduce the heat to 200°C

(400°F), Gas Mark 6. Meanwhile, whisk 2 large egg whites in a clean bowl with a hand-held electric whisk until they form soft peaks, then gradually whisk in 100 g (3½ oz) caster sugar, beating well between each addition, until the mixture is thick and glossy. Spread 175 g (6 oz) lemon curd over the pastry case, then spoon over the meringue and return the pie to the oven for 12–15 minutes until lightly golden. Serve warm or cold.

CAK-PIES-QUA

30 Fruit and Marzipan Cobbler

Serves 6–8

500 g (1 lb) mixed fruit, such as mango, plums, peach, pineapple and apricots, roughly chopped

125 g (4 oz) marzipan, coarsely grated

75 g (3 oz) plain flour, sifted

1 teaspoon baking powder

50 g (2 oz) cold unsalted butter, diced

25 g (1 oz) caster sugar

50 g (2 oz) ground almonds

pinch of salt

1 large egg, lightly beaten

toasted flaked almonds

double cream, to serve

- Gently mix together the fruit and 75 g (3 oz) of the marzipan in a bowl, then tip into a round ovenproof dish, about 20 cm (8 inches) in diameter and 4 cm (1¾ inches) deep.

- Place the flour, baking powder and butter in a food processor and pulse until the mixture resembles fine breadcrumbs. Add the sugar, ground almonds, remaining marzipan and salt and pulse until just combined. Add the egg and pulse briefly to form a soft dough.

- Top the fruit with spoonfuls of the dough and bake in a preheated oven, 200°C (400°F), Gas Mark 6, for 18–20 minutes until risen and golden. Scatter with flaked almonds and serve with cream.

 Mango and Marzipan Pots

Place 100 g (3½ oz) coarsely grated marzipan in a bowl with 200 g (7 oz) crunchy, granola-style cereal and set aside. Put 6 x 8 cm (3½ inch) shop-bought sweet pastry cases in a mini chopper or food processor and pulse briefly until crumbs. Tip into a bowl and mix with 50 g (2 oz) melted unsalted butter until well coated, then spoon into 8 serving dishes or ramekins. Place the flesh of 2 large, ripe, peeled and stoned mangoes in a food processor and blend to a purée. Fold in 200 g (7 oz) raspberries, then spoon over the crumbs and top each one with 2–3 tablespoons Greek yogurt with honey. Sprinkle over the marzipan and granola topping to serve.

 Mango and Marzipan Tartlets

Place 2 large eggs and 25 g (1 oz) caster sugar in a bowl and beat with a hand-held electric whisk until pale. Add 1 teaspoon finely grated lemon rind, 2 tablespoons lemon juice and 75 ml (3 fl oz) double cream and whisk to combine. Stir in 50 g (2 oz) finely chopped marzipan, then spoon the mixture into 8 x 8 cm (3½ inch) shop-bought sweet pastry cases on a baking sheet. Bake in a preheated oven, 200°C (400°F), Gas Mark 6, for 12 minutes, or until set. Let cool slightly on a wire rack, then top each one with 3 slices of fresh mango. Serve warm or cold.

CAK-PIES-SIT

3 Amaretti Affogato

Serves 6

2 large egg whites
150 g (5 oz) caster sugar
175 g (6 oz) ground almonds
pinch of salt
½ teaspoon almond extract
50 g (2 oz) icing sugar
22–24 whole blanched almonds
(optional)
6 scoops of good-quality vanilla
ice cream
6 shots of hot, espresso coffee

- Line 2 baking sheets with nonstick baking paper. Whisk the egg whites in a clean bowl with a hand-held electric whisk until they form stiff peaks. Mix together the sugar, ground almonds and salt in a bowl, then fold gently into the egg whites with the almond extract.

- Sift the icing sugar into a separate bowl. Roll the almond mixture into 22–24 walnut-sized balls, then roll them in the icing sugar to coat. Place on the prepared baking sheets and push 1 blanched almond, if using, gently into each.

- Bake in a preheated oven, 180°C (350°F), Gas Mark 4, for 15–18 minutes, or until cracked and pale golden. Transfer to wire racks to cool slightly.

- Scoop the ice cream into 6 espresso cups or heatproof glasses and pour 1 shot of strong, hot coffee over each. Serve immediately with the amaretti biscuits.

 Amaretti Chestnut Semifreddo

Mash together 150 g (5 oz) sweetened chestnut purée and 6 large scoops of slightly softened, good-quality vanilla ice cream in a bowl to create a rippled effect, then chill in the freezer. Meanwhile, crush 150 g (5 oz) amaretti biscuits. Divide half of the crushed biscuits between 6 serving glasses. Scoop the chilled chestnut semifreddo over the biscuits, then scatter over the remaining biscuits. Top with sliced marrons glacés, if liked. Serve immediately.

 Amaretti Chestnut Trifle

Heat 125 ml (4 fl oz) double cream in a small saucepan until almost boiling, then pour over 200 g (7 oz) finely chopped or coarsely grated plain dark chocolate in a heatproof bowl and stir until melted. Leave to cool. Meanwhile, arrange 12 soft amaretti biscuits in a trifle or glass bowl. Stir 1 tablespoon demerara sugar into 75 ml (3 fl oz) hot, strong espresso coffee until dissolved, then add 2 tablespoons amaretto liqueur. Drizzle over the biscuits, then spoon over the cooled chocolate mixture. Cover and chill for 5 minutes. Meanwhile, beat together 100 g (3½ oz) sweetened chestnut purée, 250 g (8 oz) mascarpone cheese and 100 ml (3½ fl oz) double cream in a large bowl until smooth but spreadable. Spoon evenly over the chocolate, then sprinkle with toasted flaked almonds, sliced marrons glacés or extra crushed amaretti biscuits. Serve immediately or chill until required.

Peachy Yogurt Brûlée

Serves 4

4 peaches, halved and stoned
25 g (1 oz) unsalted butter, melted
3 tablespoons soft light
   brown sugar
125 g (4 oz) Greek yogurt
75 g (3 oz) crème fraîche
½ teaspoon finely grated
   lemon rind
1 tablespoon runny honey
crushed amaretti biscuits,
   to serve

- Arrange the peaches, cut side up, in an ovenproof dish and drizzle over the melted butter, then sprinkle over the sugar. Bake in a preheated oven, 230°C (450°F), Gas Mark 8, for 6–8 minutes until lightly brûléed.

- Meanwhile, beat together the yogurt, crème fraîche, lemon rind and honey in a bowl until smooth and thick.

- Arrange the peaches on 4 serving plates and top each with a dollop of the creamy yogurt mixture. Serve immediately, sprinkled with crushed amaretti biscuits.

2 Baked Peaches with Hazelnuts

Arrange 4 stoned and quartered peaches in a ovenproof dish and sprinkle with the finely grated rind and juice of 1 orange, 50 g (2 oz) soft light brown sugar and 50 g (2 oz) chopped toasted hazelnuts. Bake in a preheated oven, 200°C (400°F), Gas Mark 6, for 15 minutes, or until softened. Meanwhile, place 25 g (1 oz) chopped or crushed hazelnuts, 50 g (2 oz) rolled oats, 25 g (1 oz) unsalted butter and 25 g (1 oz) demerara sugar in a nonstick frying pan and toast gently for 5–6 minutes, stirring frequently, until golden. Tip into a bowl to cool. Spoon the peaches and juices into 4 serving dishes, sprinkle with the hazelnut mixture and serve with dollops of Greek yogurt with honey.

3 Peach Sweetcrust Pies

Roll out 375 g (12 oz) chilled sweet pastry on a floured surface and cut out 4 x 18 cm (7 inch) rounds, rerolling the trimmings if necessary. Place on a large baking sheet lined with nonstick baking paper, then scatter 1 tablespoon fresh brown breadcrumbs over each and place half a sliced peach into the centre of each one. Mix together 50 g (2 oz) chopped toasted hazelnuts, 50 g (2 oz) soft light brown sugar, 1 teaspoon finely grated orange rind and a pinch of ground cinnamon in a bowl. Spoon over the peaches, then dot each one with a small knob of unsalted butter and fold the edges of the pastry over so that they form an open pie crust. Brush with 25 g (1 oz) melted

unsalted butter and sprinkle each one with 1 teaspoon demerara or granulated sugar. Bake in a preheated oven, 200°C (400°F), Gas Mark 6, for 18–20 minutes until crisp and golden. Serve with scoops of raspberry ripple ice cream.

CAK-PIES-TEP

3 Blueberry and Mandarin Puffs

Serves 4

butter, for greasing
6 trifle sponge fingers, halved
200 g (7 oz) canned mandarin
   segments in juice, drained
2 teaspoons grated orange rind
125 g (4 oz) blueberries
3 tablespoons soft dark
   brown sugar
2 tablespoons chopped toasted
   hazelnuts
125 g (4 oz) chilled puff pastry
flour, for dusting
beaten egg, to glaze
25 g (1 oz) vanilla sugar
mascarpone cheese, to serve

For the blueberry sauce

150 g (5 oz) blueberries
50 g (2 oz) vanilla sugar
1 teaspoon finely grated orange rind
1 teaspoon vanilla extract
2 tablespoons freshly squeezed
   orange juice
1 teaspoon vanilla extract

- Lightly grease 4 x 200 ml (7 fl oz) ramekins, then divide the sponge fingers between them. Mix together the mandarins, orange rind, blueberries, brown sugar and hazelnuts in a bowl, then spoon over the sponge fingers.

- Roll out the pastry on a floured surface and cut out 4 x 10 cm (4 inch) rounds. Lay over the ramekins and press the edges to seal. Cut a cross in each top, then brush with beaten egg and sprinkle with the vanilla sugar. Bake in a preheated oven, 220°C (425°F), Gas Mark 7, for 15 minutes, or until puffed and golden.

- Meanwhile, make the blueberry sauce. Place all the ingredients in a small saucepan and heat gently, stirring occasionally, until the sugar has dissolved. Simmer gently for 1–2 minutes until the fruit has collapsed, then leave to cool slightly.

- Serve the blueberry and mandarin puffs spooned into 4 bowls with the puff pastry on top. Drizzle with the warm sauce and serve with dollops of mascarpone. Alternatively, serve directly from the ramekins.

 Blueberry Cream Flan

Spread 125 g (4 oz) blueberry jam over 1 medium sponge flan base. Beat together 125 ml (4 fl oz) double cream, 200 g (7 oz) mascarpone cheese and 50 g (2 oz) vanilla sugar until thick and smooth. Spoon over the jam, then scatter over 200 g (7 oz) blueberries. Serve immediately.

 Jammy Blueberry Tarts

Unroll a 375 g (12 oz) pack chilled ready-rolled puff pastry and stamp out 12 rounds using an 8 cm (3½ inch) plain cutter. Push into a 12-hole shallow bun tray, then fill each one with 1 teaspoon blueberry jam. Bake in a preheated oven, 220°C (425°F), Gas Mark 7, for 12 minutes, or

until puffed and golden. Meanwhile, beat together 50 ml (2 fl oz) double cream, 100 g (3½ oz) mascarpone cheese and 15 g (½ oz) vanilla sugar until thick and smooth. Let the tarts cool slightly on a wire rack, then top each with a dollop of vanilla cream and 2–3 blueberries.

CAK-PIES-QAI

QuickCook
Muffins and Cupcakes

Recipes listed by cooking time

30

20

10

30 Victoria Sponge Cupcakes

Makes 6

75 g (3 oz) unsalted butter,
softened, plus extra for greasing

75 g (3 oz) golden caster sugar,
plus extra for sprinkling

75 g (3 oz) self-raising flour,
sifted

1 large egg, lightly beaten

1 tablespoon milk

½ teaspoon vanilla extract

6 teaspoons strawberry or
raspberry jam

For the icing

50 g (2 oz) unsalted butter,
softened

100 g (3½ oz) icing sugar, sifted

½ teaspoon vanilla extract

- Grease a 12-hole nonstick muffin tin. Place the butter, sugar, flour, egg, milk and vanilla extract in a large bowl and beat together with a hand-held electric whisk until pale and creamy.

- Spoon the mixture into the prepared muffin tin and bake in a preheated oven, 200°C (400°F), Gas Mark 6, for 8–10 minutes until golden and firm to the touch. Transfer to a wire rack, placing half of the cakes top side down, and leave to cool completely.

- Meanwhile, make the icing. Place all the ingredients in a small bowl and beat with a hand-held electric whisk until light and fluffy. Spoon into a piping bag fitted with a star-shaped nozzle or use a small palette knife for spreading.

- Pipe or spread the icing over the 6 flat-sided cupcakes, then top each with 1 teaspoon of the jam. Top with the remaining cupcakes, rounded side up. Serve sprinkled with caster sugar.

---

1 Victoria Sandwich Muffins

Cut 4 shop-bought vanilla muffins in half horizontally. Whip 75 ml (3 fl oz) double cream and ½ teaspoon vanilla bean paste in a bowl with a hand-held electric whisk until it forms soft peaks. Spread 1 teaspoon strawberry or raspberry jam over the muffin bases, then top with the cream and replace the tops. Serve sprinkled with caster sugar.

2 Jammy Victoria Cupcakes

Place 125 g (4 oz) each of softened unsalted butter, caster sugar and sifted self-raising flour and 2 large lightly beaten eggs in a large bowl and beat with a hand-held electric whisk until pale and creamy. Spoon the mixture into a 12-hole nonstick muffin tin lined with paper cupcake cases and bake in a preheated oven, 200°C (400°F), Gas Mark 6, for 12–14 minutes until risen and golden. Transfer to a wire rack to cool for a few minutes. Cut off the tops of the cupcakes, then fill each dip with 1 teaspoon strawberry or raspberry jam and replace the tops. Serve dusted with icing sugar.

CAK-MUFF-FYO

30 Cinnamon and Apple Cookie Crumble Muffins

Makes 12

250 g (8 oz) plain flour
1 teaspoon baking powder
1 teaspoon bicarbonate of soda
1 teaspoon ground cinnamon
pinch of salt
125 g (4 oz) soft light brown sugar
2 large eggs, lightly beaten
150 ml (¼ pint) buttermilk
50 g (2 oz) unsalted butter, melted
175 g (6 oz) shop-bought apple purée
1 small dessert apple, peeled, cored and coarsely grated
200 g (7 oz) shop-bought chilled cookie dough, chopped or crumbled

- Line a 12-hole nonstick muffin tin with paper muffin cases or lightly grease. Sift the flour, baking powder, bicarbonate of soda, cinnamon and salt into a large bowl, then stir in the sugar.

- Beat together the eggs, buttermilk, melted butter, apple purée, grated apple and half of the cookie dough in a large bowl. Add to the dry ingredients and stir until just combined.

- Spoon the mixture into the prepared muffin tin and crumble the remaining cookie dough over the tops.

- Bake in a preheated oven, 180°C (350°F), Gas Mark 4, for 18–22 minutes until risen and golden. Serve warm.

---

 1 Cookie Dough Cupcake Sundaes

Cut out deep circles from the tops of 4 shop-bought large chocolate cupcakes and reserve. Place the cakes in 4 serving dishes, fill each dip with 1 scoop of cookie dough ice cream and drizzle over 150 g (5 oz) warmed shop-bought Belgian chocolate sauce. Crumble over the reserved cupcake tops and 4 chocolate chip cookies, then dust each with 1 teaspoon cinnamon sugar. Serve immediately with whipped cream.

 2 Cinnamon Cookie Dough Cupcakes

Place 125 g (4 oz) each of softened unsalted butter, soft light brown sugar and sifted self-raising flour, 1 teaspoon ground cinnamon, 2 large lightly beaten eggs and 100 g (3½ oz) shop-bought chilled cookie dough, chopped, in a large bowl and beat together with a hand-held electric whisk until combined. Spoon the mixture into a 12-hole nonstick muffin tin lined with paper cupcakes cases and bake in a preheated oven,

200°C (400°F), Gas Mark 6, for 12–14 minutes until risen and firm to the touch. Transfer to wire racks to cool slightly, then serve warm dusted with cinnamon sugar, if liked.

CAK-MUFF-RAF

Turkish Delight Cakes with Rosewater Cream

Makes 18

150 g (5 oz) unsalted butter, melted and cooled, plus extra for greasing
3 large egg whites
pinch of salt
100 g (3½ oz) ground almonds
100 g (3½ oz) plain flour, sifted
150 g (5 oz) caster sugar
1 teaspoon rosewater
75 g (3 oz) rose-flavoured Turkish delight, chopped
edible rose petals, to decorate

For the rosewater cream

200 ml (7 fl oz) double cream
1 teaspoon rosewater
½ teaspoon vanilla bean paste or extract
4 tablespoons icing sugar, sifted

- Lightly brush 18 holes of 2 x 12-hole silicone friand trays, madeleine trays or mini muffin tins with melted butter.

- Whisk the egg whites and salt in a large, clean bowl with a hand-held electric whisk until they form soft peaks, then gently fold in the ground almonds, flour and sugar. Fold in the melted butter, rosewater and Turkish delight.

- Spoon the mixture into the prepared tins and bake in a preheated oven, 220°C (425°F), Gas Mark 7, for 8–10 minutes until risen and golden.

- Meanwhile, make the rosewater cream. Whip all the ingredients in a bowl with a hand-held electric whisk until soft peaks form, then place in a serving bowl.

- Remove the cakes from the oven and transfer to a wire rack to cool slightly. Serve with dollops of the rosewater cream and decorated with edible rose petals.

 Rosewater Cream Butterfly Cakes

Make half a quantity of the Rosewater Cream as above. Cut out deep circles from the tops of 12 shop-bought vanilla or strawberry cupcakes, then cut each top in half. Fill the dips in the cupcakes with the cream, then replace the tops, positioning to resemble butterfly wings. Dust with icing sugar and scatter with pale pink, edible rose petals, if liked.

 Turkish Delight Muffins

Sift 200 g (7 oz) plain flour, 2 teaspoons baking powder and 1 teaspoon bicarbonate of soda into a large bowl, then stir in 75 g (3 oz) ground almonds, 100 g (3½ oz) caster sugar and 75 g (3 oz) diced rose-flavoured Turkish delight. Whisk together 2 large lightly beaten eggs, 1 teaspoon rosewater, 150 ml (¼ pint) buttermilk and 50 ml (2 fl oz) vegetable oil in a jug.

Pour into the dry ingredients and stir until just combined. Spoon the mixture into a greased or muffin case-lined 12-holed nonstick muffin tin and scatter over an extra 75 g (3 oz) diced Turkish delight. Bake in a preheated oven, 180°C (350°F), Gas Mark 4, for 18–22 minutes until risen and golden. Meanwhile, make the Rosewater Cream as above. Serve with the warm muffins and decorate with edible rose petals, if liked.

CAK-MUFF-MAT

30 Upside-Down Pineapple and Apricot Muffins

Serves 6

butter, for greasing
150 g (5 oz) canned pineapple
  or apricots in juice, drained
  and diced
3 tablespoons maple syrup
250 g (8 oz) self-raising flour
1 teaspoon bicarbonate of soda
pinch of salt
100 g (3½ oz) soft light
  brown sugar
75 g (3 oz) dried pineapple,
  chopped
1 large egg, lightly beaten
75 ml (3 fl oz) vegetable oil
150 ml (¼ pint) buttermilk
2 tablespoons apricot jam
1 teaspoon grated orange rind
ice cream or custard, to serve

- Generously grease a 6-hole giant muffin tin, each hole about 10 x 5 cm (4 x 2 inches). Divide the diced pineapple or apricot between the holes and drizzle over the maple syrup.

- Sift the flour, bicarbonate of soda and salt into a large bowl, then stir in the sugar and dried pineapple. Whisk together the remaining ingredients in a jug. Pour into the dry ingredients and stir until just combined.

- Spoon the mixture into the prepared muffin tin and bake in a preheated oven, 180°C (350°F), Gas Mark 4, for 22 minutes, or until risen, golden and firm to the touch.

- Invert the muffins on to 6 serving dishes and serve with ice cream or custard.

 1 Pineapple and Mango Muffin Trifle Cut 3 shop-bought lemon muffins into cubes and place in a bowl. Drizzle over 75 ml (3 fl oz) tropical fruit juice, then top with 1 sliced ripe mango and ½ chopped pineapple. Pour over 300 g (10 oz) shop-bought fresh custard. Whip 200 ml (7 fl oz) double cream and 2 tablespoons vanilla sugar in a large bowl with a hand-held electric whisk until it forms soft peaks, then spoon over the custard. Serve scattered with 25 g (1 oz) toasted chopped hazelnuts.

 2 Pineapple and Mango Cupcakes Place 125 g (4 oz) each of softened unsalted butter, golden caster sugar and sifted plain flour, 2 teaspoons baking powder, ½ teaspoon bicarbonate of soda, 1 teaspoon finely grated orange rind and 2 large lightly beaten eggs in a bowl and beat together with a hand-held electric whisk until pale and creamy. Fold in 75 g (3 oz) mixed ready-to-eat dried pineapple and mango, chopped. Spoon the mixture into a 12-hole nonstick muffin tin lined with paper cupcake cases and bake in a preheated oven, 200°C (400°F), Gas Mark 6, for 12–15 minutes until risen and golden. Transfer to a wire rack to cool slightly, then serve warm

Blueberry and Vanilla Iced Cupcakes

Makes 12

12 shop-bought vanilla cupcakes
100 g (3½ oz) blueberries
purple sugar sprinkles, to
    decorate (optional)

For the icing

75 g (3 oz) unsalted butter,
    softened
100 g (3½ oz) icing sugar, sifted
200 g (7 oz) mascarpone cheese
1 teaspoon finely grated lemon
    rind
seeds scraped from 1 vanilla pod
    or 1 teaspoon vanilla bean paste

- To make the icing, place the butter and icing sugar in a bowl and beat together with a hand-held electric whisk until light and fluffy. Add the mascarpone, lemon rind and vanilla seeds or paste and beat until smooth, taking care not to over-beat as the mixture will split.

- Spoon the icing into a piping bag fitted with a star-shaped piping nozzle, then pipe over the cupcakes.

- Decorate with the blueberries, then serve sprinkled with purple sugar sprinkles, if liked.

Blueberry Swirl Mini Muffins

Sift 125 g (4 oz) self-raising flour, ¼ teaspoon bicarbonate of soda and a pinch of salt into a large bowl, then stir in 50 g (2 oz) golden caster sugar. Whisk together 1 large lightly beaten egg, 1 teaspoon lemon juice, 1 teaspoon grated lemon rind, 25 g (1 oz) melted unsalted butter and 75 ml (3 fl oz) buttermilk in a jug. Pour into the dry ingredients, add 2 tablespoons blueberry jam and stir until just combined. Spoon the mixture into a greased or case-lined 12-hole mini muffin tin and bake in a preheated oven, 200°C (400°F), Gas Mark 6, for 12–15 minutes until risen and golden. Serve warm.

Mascarpone Berry Cupcakes

Beat together 100 g (3½ oz) mascarpone cheese, ½ teaspoon vanilla bean paste or extract and 2 teaspoons caster sugar in a bowl until smooth and set aside. Place 3 large lightly beaten eggs, 150 g (5 oz) golden caster sugar, 100 g (3½ oz) softened unsalted butter, 50 g (2 oz) mascarpone, 1 teaspoon vanilla extract, 175 g (6 oz) sifted self-raising flour and ½ teaspoon baking powder in a separate bowl and beat together with a hand-held electric whisk until pale and creamy. Fold in 75 g (3 oz) blueberries. Spoon the mixture into a 12-hole nonstick muffin tin lined with paper cupcake cases, then make a deep dip in each and fill the dips with 1 small spoonful of the mascarpone cream. Bake in a preheated oven, 200°C (400°F), Gas Mark 6, for 18–20 minutes until risen and golden. Leave to cool in the tin for 1–2 minutes, then transfer to a wire rack to cool slightly. Serve warm.

CAK-MUFF-VEE

 **Honeyed Cherry Friands**

Makes 12

125 g (4 oz) unsalted butter, melted and cooled, plus extra for greasing
4 large egg whites
75 g (3 oz) plain flour
150 g (5 oz) icing sugar
100 g (3½ oz) ground hazelnuts
pinch of salt
75 g (3 oz) dried cherries
warmed honey, to serve

- Lightly brush a 12-hole friand or mini muffin tin with melted butter.

- Whisk the egg whites in a large, clean bowl with a hand-held electric whisk until frothy and foamy, but not stiff. Sift in the flour and icing sugar, then add the hazelnuts and salt and gently fold in until just combined. Fold in the melted butter and dried cherries.

- Spoon the mixture into the prepared tin and bake in a preheated oven, 200°C (400°F), Gas Mark 6, for 12–14 minutes until golden and firm to the touch.

- Leave to cool in the tin for 1–2 minutes, then transfer to a wire rack to cool slightly. Serve drizzled with warmed honey.

 Cherry Compote Cupcakes

Place 50 g (2 oz) caster sugar, 50 ml (2 fl oz) orange juice, 125 g (4 oz) pitted fresh or frozen cherries, 1 teaspoon almond extract and 1 teaspoon finely grated orange rind in a saucepan and heat gently, stirring occasionally, until the sugar has dissolved. Increase the heat and simmer gently for 4–5 minutes until the cherries are soft and syrupy. Meanwhile, place 6 warmed shop-bought vanilla cupcakes in 6 serving dishes and top each one with a dollop of crème fraîche or ice cream. Spoon over the warm cherry compote and serve immediately.

 Honey and Sour Cherry Muffins

Sift 200 g (7 oz) self-raising flour, 1 teaspoon baking powder and a pinch of salt into a large bowl, then stir in 100 g (3½ oz) ground almonds, 125 g (4 oz) caster sugar, 75 g (3 oz) sour cherries and 2 teaspoons finely grated orange rind. Whisk together 2 large lightly beaten eggs, 50 ml (2 fl oz) vegetable oil, 2 tablespoons runny honey, 100 ml (3½ fl oz) milk and 100 g (3½ oz) Greek yogurt in a jug. Pour into the dry ingredients and stir until just combined. Spoon the mixture into a greased or muffin case-lined 12-hole nonstick muffin tin and bake in a preheated oven, 180°C (350°F), Gas Mark 4, for 18–22 minutes until risen and golden. Serve warm.

1 Lemony Poppy Seed Frosted Muffins

Makes 4

4 shop-bought jumbo lemon and poppy seed muffins
sugared lemon slices, to decorate

For the frosting

100 g (3½ oz) cream cheese
25 g (1 oz) unsalted butter, softened
75 g (3 oz) icing sugar, sifted
1 teaspoon lemon juice
1 teaspoon finely grated lemon rind

- To make the frosting, place all the ingredients in a large bowl and beat together until thick and smooth.

- Spoon a large dollop of icing on top of each muffin and decorate with the lemon slices.

2 Lemon and Poppy Seed Cupcakes

Beat together 125 g (4 oz) each of softened unsalted butter, caster sugar and sifted self-raising flour, 1 tablespoon poppy seeds, 2 large lightly beaten eggs, 1 tablespoon milk and 1 teaspoon grated lemon rind with a hand-held electric whisk until pale and creamy. Spoon the mixture into a 12-hole muffin tin lined with paper cupcake cases and bake in a preheated oven, 200 °C (400 °F), Gas Mark 6, for 12–15 minutes until risen and golden. Meanwhile, mix together 1 tablespoon each of lemon juice, water and caster sugar. Drizzle over the warm cupcakes and leave to cool slightly.

3 Lemon Drizzle Poppy Seed

Muffins Sift 250 g (8 oz) plain flour, 2 teaspoons baking powder, ½ teaspoon bicarbonate of soda and a pinch of salt into a large bowl, then stir in 2 tablespoons poppy seeds, 2 teaspoons finely grated lemon rind and 125 g (4 oz) caster sugar. Whisk together 2 large lightly beaten eggs, 2 teaspoons lemon juice, 50 g (2 oz) melted unsalted butter and 150 ml (¼ pint) buttermilk in a jug. Pour into the dry ingredients and stir until just combined. Spoon the mixture into a greased or muffin case-lined 12-hole nonstick muffin tin and bake in a preheated oven, 180 °C (350 °F),

Gas Mark 4, for 18–22 minutes until risen and golden. Meanwhile, gently heat 50 g (2 oz) caster sugar and 2 tablespoons water in a small saucepan until dissolved, then increase the heat and simmer gently for 2–3 minutes until syrupy. Remove from the heat and stir in 1 tablespoon lemon juice. Drizzle over the warm muffins and leave to cool slightly before serving.

AK-MUFF-XOZ

Spiced Ginger Cupcakes

Makes 12

150 g (5 oz) unsalted butter,
  softened
125 g (4 oz) soft dark brown
  sugar
1 tablespoon runny honey
3 large eggs, lightly beaten
150 g (5 oz) plain flour
2 teaspoons baking powder
1 teaspoon ground ginger
pinch of ground cloves

For the icing

50 g (2 oz) icing sugar, sifted
15 g (½ oz) piece of stem ginger
  in syrup, drained and cut into
  thin matchsticks
1 tablespoon stem ginger syrup
  (taken from the jar)
½ teaspoon water

- Line a 12-hole nonstick muffin tin with paper cupcake cases. Place the butter, sugar, honey and eggs in a large bowl, then sift in the flour, baking powder, ground ginger and cloves. Beat together with a hand-held electric whisk until the mixture is pale and creamy.

- Spoon the mixture into the prepared muffin tin and bake in a preheated oven, 200°C (400°F), Gas Mark 6, for 12–15 minutes until risen and firm to the touch.

- Meanwhile, make the icing. Mix together all the ingredients in a small bowl until runny and smooth.

- Remove the cupcakes from the oven, then transfer to a wire rack and drizzle over the ginger icing. Serve warm or cold.

Ginger Iced Muffins
Mix together 125 g
(4 oz) sifted icing sugar,
1 teaspoon ground ginger,
1 tablespoon stem ginger syrup
and 1 teaspoon lemon juice
in a small bowl until thick
but spreadable. Spread over
4 shop-bought large raisin or
lemon muffins, then decorate
each one with a wafer-thin slice
of drained stem ginger in syrup.

Moist Ginger Muffins
Sift 200 g (7 oz) self-raising
flour, 1 teaspoon baking powder
and 1 teaspoon ground ginger
into a large bowl, then stir in
100 g (3½ oz) ground almonds
and 150 g (5 oz) soft dark brown
sugar. Beat together 1 large
lightly beaten egg, 75 g (3 oz)
melted unsalted butter,
1 tablespoon black treacle,
2 x 15 g (½ oz) pieces of stem
ginger, chopped, 50 g (2 oz)
golden syrup, 75 g (3 oz) crème
fraîche and 125 ml (4 fl oz) milk
in a large jug or bowl. Pour
into the dry ingredients and
stir until just combined. Spoon
the mixture into a greased
or muffin case-lined 12-hole
nonstick muffin tin and bake in a
preheated oven, 180°C (350°F),
Gas Mark 4, for 18–22 minutes
until risen and firm to the touch.
Serve warm.

30 White Chocolate and Raspberry Bran Muffins

Makes 12

200 g (7 oz) plain wholemeal flour
2 teaspoons baking powder
pinch of salt
50 g (2 oz) soft dark brown sugar
25 g (1 oz) bran
75 g (3 oz) white chocolate
 chunks
2 large eggs, lightly beaten
50 g (2 oz) unsalted butter,
 melted
125 ml (4 fl oz) buttermilk
1 ripe banana, mashed
50 g (2 oz) frozen raspberries,
 crumbled
12 sweetened dried banana chips

- Line a 12-hole nonstick muffin tin with paper muffin cases or lightly grease. Sift the flour, baking powder and salt into a large bowl, then stir in the sugar, bran and chocolate chunks.

- Beat together the eggs, melted butter, buttermilk and banana in a jug. Pour into the dry ingredients, add the raspberries and stir until just combined.

- Spoon the mixture into the prepared muffin tin and top each muffin with a banana chip. Bake in a preheated oven, 180°C (350°F), Gas Mark 4, for 18–22 minutes until risen and firm to the touch. Serve warm.

10 White Choc and Raspberry Sponges Heat 100 ml (3½ fl oz) double cream in small saucepan until almost boiling, then pour over 150 g (5 oz) finely chopped white chocolate in a heatproof bowl and stir until melted. Leave to cool. Cut 8 shop-bought vanilla cupcakes in half horizontally. Beat 75 g (3 oz) mascarpone cheese into the cooled cream, then fold in 75 g (3 oz) raspberries and spread over the cupcake bases. Sandwich together with the tops. Serve immediately.

20 White Choc and Raspberry Cupcakes Place 125 g (4 oz) softened unsalted butter, 125 g (4 oz) caster sugar, 100 g (3½ oz) sifted self-raising flour, 50 g (2 oz) ground almonds, 2 large lightly beaten eggs and ½ teaspoon vanilla extract in a large bowl and beat together with a hand-held electric whisk until pale and creamy. Fold in 75 g (3 oz) white chocolate chips and 50 g (2 oz) crumbled, frozen raspberries. Spoon into a 12-hole nonstick muffin tin lined with paper cupcake cases and bake in a preheated oven, 200°C (400°F), Gas Mark 6, for 12–15 minutes until risen and golden. Transfer to a wire rack to cool. Serve decorated with fresh raspberries and white chocolate curls.

CAK-MUFF-GOW

20 Apricot and Orange Friands

Makes 12

175 g (6 oz) unsalted butter, melted and cooled, plus extra for greasing
5 large egg whites
1 teaspoon finely grated orange rind
1 teaspoon orange extract
75 g (3 oz) plain flour
200 g (7 oz) icing sugar
125 g (4 oz) ground almonds
pinch of salt
50 g (2 oz) ready-to-eat semi-dried apricots, chopped

- Lightly brush a 12-hole friand or mini muffin tin with melted butter.

- Whisk the egg whites, orange rind and extract in a large, clean bowl with a hand-held electric whisk until frothy and foamy, but not stiff. Sift in the flour and icing sugar, then add the ground almonds and salt and gently fold in. Fold in the melted butter and apricots.

- Spoon the mixture into the prepared tin and bake in a preheated oven, 220°C (425°F), Gas Mark 7, for 12–14 minutes until risen and golden. Transfer to a wire rack to cool.

 Syrupy Apricot and Orange Muffins

Remove the rind from 1–2 large unwaxed oranges in thin strips and heat gently in a small saucepan with 75 g (3 oz) caster sugar and 75 ml (3 fl oz) orange juice until the sugar has dissolved. Add 50 g (2 oz) chopped ready-to-eat semi-dried apricots, increase the heat and simmer gently for 3–4 minutes until slightly syrupy. Pour into a jug to cool slightly. Place 4 warmed shop-bought cinnamon, raisin or plain muffins in 4 serving dishes and pour over the syrup. Serve with Greek yogurt and chopped pistachio nuts, if liked.

 Orangey Apricot Cranberry Muffins

Sift 250 g (8 oz) wholemeal self-raising flour, 1 teaspoon baking powder, ½ teaspoon bicarbonate of soda, ½ teaspoon ground cinnamon and a pinch of salt into a large bowl, then stir in 100 g (3½ oz) soft light brown sugar, 75 g (3 oz) dried cranberries and 75 g (3 oz) chopped ready-to-eat semi-dried apricots. Whisk together 2 large lightly beaten eggs, 175 ml (6 fl oz) buttermilk, 50 ml (2 fl oz) vegetable oil and 1 teaspoon orange extract in a jug. Pour into the dry ingredients and stir until just combined.

Spoon the mixture into a greased or muffin case-lined 12-hole nonstick muffin tin and bake in a preheated oven, 180°C (350°F), Gas Mark 4, for 18–22 minutes until risen and golden. Serve warm.

30 Date and Fudge Muffins

Makes 12

175 g (6 oz) plain flour
2 teaspoons baking powder
½ teaspoon bicarbonate of soda
pinch of salt
75 g (3 oz) rolled oats
75 g (3 oz) baking fudge chunks
2 large eggs, lightly beaten
50 g (2 oz) unsalted butter,
  melted
100 g (3½ oz) pitted dates,
  chopped
100 g (3½ oz) runny honey
150 g (5 oz) Greek yogurt
75 ml (3 fl oz) milk

- Line a 12-hole nonstick muffin tin with paper muffin cases or lightly grease. Sift the plain flour, baking powder, bicarbonate of soda and salt into a large bowl, then stir in the oats and fudge chunks.

- Beat together the remaining ingredients in a jug or bowl. Pour into the dry ingredients and stir until just combined.

- Spoon the mixture into the prepared muffin tin and bake in a preheated oven, 180°C (350°F), Gas Mark 4, for 18–22 minutes until risen, golden and firm to the touch. Serve warm.

10 Fudgy Date Muffins

Place 50 g (2 oz) unsalted butter, 2 tablespoons golden syrup, 25 g (1 oz) soft dark brown sugar, 75 g (3 oz) chopped pitted dates, 75 g (3 oz) chopped walnuts and 4 tablespoons double cream in a small saucepan and heat gently until the butter has melted and the sugar dissolved. Bring to the boil, then pour into a jug to cool slightly. Meanwhile, place 4 warmed shop-bought large banana or toffee-flavoured muffins in 4 serving dishes. Drizzle over the fudgy date sauce and serve with whipped or clotted cream.

20 Date and Fudge Cupcakes

Place 125 g (4 oz) each of softened unsalted butter, caster sugar and sifted self-raising flour, ½ teaspoon baking powder, 1 teaspoon coffee essence and 2 large lightly beaten eggs in a large bowl and beat together with a hand-held electric whisk until pale and creamy. Fold in 50 g (2 oz) finely chopped pitted dates and 50 g (2 oz) chopped walnuts. Spoon the mixture into a 12-hole nonstick muffin tin lined with paper cupcake cases, then scatter over 50 g (2 oz) baking fudge chunks. Bake in a preheated oven, 200°C (400°F), Gas Mark 6, for 12–15 minutes until risen and golden. Meanwhile, place 75 g (3 oz) softened unsalted butter, 125 g (4 oz) sifted icing sugar and 1 teaspoon coffee essence in a bowl and beat together with a hand-held electric whisk until light and fluffy. Serve the cupcakes warm with the coffee buttercream.

2 Peppermint Cupcakes

Makes 12

2 tablespoons cocoa powder

2 tablespoons boiling water

½ teaspoon peppermint extract

100 g (3½ oz) unsalted butter, softened

125 g (4 oz) caster sugar

125 g (4 oz) self-raising flour, sifted

1 teaspoon baking powder

2 large eggs, lightly beaten

1 tablespoon milk

75 g (3 oz) mint-flavoured plain dark chocolate, chopped

• Line a 12-hole nonstick muffin tin with paper cupcake cases or lightly grease. Place the cocoa powder in a small bowl, then stir in the boiling water and peppermint extract until smooth. Set aside.

• Place the butter, sugar, flour, baking powder, eggs and milk in a large bowl and beat together with a hand-held electric whisk until pale and creamy. Scrape in the chocolate paste and beat until smooth, then stir in the chopped chocolate.

• Spoon the mixture into the prepared muffin tin and bake in a preheated oven, 200°C (400°F), Gas Mark 6, for 12–14 minutes until risen and firm. Transfer to a wire rack to cool slightly, then serve warm.

---

1 Peppermint Cream Cupcakes

Place 150 g (5 oz) softened unsalted butter, 225 g (7½ oz) sifted icing sugar and ½ teaspoon peppermint extract in a large bowl and beat together with a hand-held electric whisk until light and fluffy. If liked, colour the buttercream with a drop of green food colouring, then beat well to combine. Spoon the icing into a piping bag fitted with a star-shaped nozzle, then pipe over 12 shop-bought chocolate cupcakes.

3 Mint Choc Chip Muffins

Sift 275 g (9 oz) plain flour, 3 tablespoons cocoa powder, 1 teaspoon baking powder, 1 teaspoon bicarbonate of soda and a pinch of salt into a large bowl, then stir in 175 g (6 oz) caster sugar and 100 g (3½ oz) mint-flavoured plain dark chocolate, chopped. Whisk together 3 large lightly beaten eggs, ½ teaspoon peppermint extract, 75 ml (3 fl oz) vegetable oil and 200 ml (7 fl oz) milk in a jug. Pour into the dry ingredients and stir until just combined. Spoon the mixture into a greased or muffin case-lined 12-hole nonstick muffin tin. Bake in a preheated oven, 180°C (350°F), Gas Mark 4, for 18–22 minutes until risen and firm to the touch. Serve warm.

CAK-MUFF-XOI

3⓪ Maple and Macadamia Madeleines

Makes 18

2 large eggs

100 g (3½ oz) caster sugar

2 tablespoons maple syrup, plus
extra to serve (optional)

pinch of salt

125 g (4 oz) plain flour, plus extra
for dusting

½ teaspoon baking powder

50 g (2 oz) macadamia nuts, very
finely chopped

125 g (4 oz) unsalted butter,
melted and cooled, plus extra
for greasing

- Place the eggs, sugar, maple syrup and salt in a large bowl and beat with a hand-held electric whisk until pale and thick and doubled in volume. Sift in the flour and baking powder, then add the macadamia nuts and melted butter and fold in until combined. Cover and chill for at least 10 minutes. (This helps the traditional 'bump' to form in the centre of each madeleine.)

- Meanwhile, grease 18 holes of 2 x 12-hole madeleine trays with melted butter, then dust lightly with flour, tapping the tin to remove any excess.

- Gently stir the madeleine mixture, then spoon into the prepared trays until each hole is about three-quarters full. Bake in a preheated oven, 220°C (425°F), Gas Mark 7, for 3 minutes, then reduce the oven temperature to 200°C (400°F), Gas Mark 6, and bake for a further 4–6 minutes until risen and golden.

- Transfer to a wire rack to cool slightly, then serve warm drizzled with extra warmed maple syrup, if liked.

 **Maple Butter
Petits Fours**

Toast 75 g (3 oz) halved macadamia nuts in a dry frying pan until golden. Tip on to a plate to cool. Meanwhile, beat together 125 g (4 oz) softened butter, 250 g (8 oz) sifted icing sugar and 2 tablespoons maple syrup until light and fluffy. Cut 1 shop-bought large plain sponge cake into bite-sized squares. Pipe a swirl of icing on to each square and top with the toasted nuts.

 **Maple-Drizzled
Whoopies**

Beat together 50 g (2 oz) softened unsalted butter, 50 g (2 oz) caster sugar, 25 g (1 oz) soft light brown sugar and a pinch of salt until light and fluffy. Add 1 large egg yolk, 2 teaspoons maple syrup and 50 ml (2 fl oz) buttermilk, then sift in 100 g (3½ oz) self-raising flour and beat until combined. Pipe or spoon the mixture into a greased 24-hole whoopie pie tin. Bake in a preheated oven, 200°C

(400°F), Gas Mark 6, for 10 minutes, or until risen and firm to the touch. Serve warm drizzled with warmed maple syrup and scattered with crushed macadamia nuts.

Peanut Butter and Chocolate Mini Muffins

Makes 12

25 g (1 oz) unsalted butter
100 g (3½ oz) crunchy
   peanut butter
150 g (5 oz) plain flour
1½ teaspoons baking powder
pinch of salt
75 g (3 oz) soft light brown sugar
1 large egg, lightly beaten
125 ml (4 fl oz) buttermilk
50 g (2 oz) milk chocolate chunks
   or chips

- Line a 12-hole mini muffin tin with paper mini muffin cases or lightly grease. Place the butter and peanut butter in a small saucepan over a low heat and warm until just melted. Stir gently, then set aside.

- Meanwhile, sift the flour, baking powder and salt into a large bowl, then stir in the sugar. Whisk together the egg, buttermilk and melted butters in a jug. Pour into the dry ingredients and stir until just combined.

- Spoon the mixture into the prepared muffin tin, then scatter over the chocolate chunks or chips.

- Bake in a preheated oven, 200°C (400°F), Gas Mark 6, for 10–15 minutes until risen and golden. Serve warm.

 Peanut and Choc Muffin Cups

Place 50 g (2 oz) blanched unsalted peanuts in a dry frying pan and toast over a medium-low heat, shaking frequently, until golden. Tip on to a plate to cool. Meanwhile, spoon 1 tablespoon shop-bought Belgian chocolate sauce into each of 4 flat-bottomed ice-cream cups or cones. Cut 2 chilled shop-bought chocolate muffins into cubes and divide between the cups. Top each with 1 scoop of chocolate or chocolate fudge brownie ice cream and 1 swirl of aerosol whipped cream. Place the peanuts in a freezer bag and tap lightly with a rolling pin until crushed, then scatter over the cream. Serve immediately.

 Peanut and Chocolate Melt Muffins Make double the quantity of the mini muffin mixture as above. Spoon half the mixture into a greased or muffin case-lined 12-hole nonstick muffin tin and drop 1 teaspoon chocolate spread or 1 large chocolate chunk on to each one. Top with the remaining mixture and bake in a preheated oven, 180°C (350°F), Gas Mark 4, for 18–22 minutes until risen and firm to the touch. Serve warm.

CAK-MUFF-QYV

3 Chocolate Orange Madeleines

Makes 12

75 g (3 oz) butter, melted and cooled, plus extra for greasing

75 g (3 oz) self-raising flour, plus extra for dusting

2 large eggs

1 teaspoon orange extract

1 teaspoon finely grated orange rind

75 g (3 oz) caster sugar

pinch of salt

100 g (3½ oz) plain dark or milk chocolate, broken into small pieces

- Lightly brush a 12-hole silicone madeleine tray, friand tray or mini muffin tin with melted butter and dust lightly with flour.

- Place the eggs, orange extract, orange rind, sugar and salt in a large bowl and beat with a hand-held electric hand whisk until pale and thick and the whisk leaves a trail when lifted above the mixture. Sift in the flour, then add the melted butter and fold gently until combined.

- Spoon the mixture into the prepared tray and bake in a preheated oven, 200°C (400°F), Gas Mark 6, for 8–10 minutes until risen and golden.

- Meanwhile, melt the chocolate in a heatproof bowl set over a saucepan of gently simmering water, ensuring the bowl does not touch the water. Stir gently and set aside.

- Remove the madeleines from the oven and transfer to a wire rack. Once cool to the touch, spread some melted chocolate over each cake. Leave to set in a cool place for a few minutes before serving.

 Chocolate Orange Cream Cupcakes

Melt 125 g (4 oz) orange-flavoured milk chocolate, 50 ml (2 fl oz) double cream and 50 g (2 oz) unsalted butter in a small saucepan, then scrape into a bowl and beat in 75 g (3 oz) sifted icing sugar and 1 teaspoon orange extract until thick and smooth. Spread over 12 shop-bought plain cupcakes.

 Choc Chip and Orange Cupcakes

Place 125 g (4 oz) softened unsalted butter, 125 g (4 oz) caster sugar, 150 g (5 oz) sifted self-raising flour, ½ teaspoon baking powder, 1 teaspoon finely grated orange rind, ½ teaspoon orange extract and 2 large lightly beaten eggs in a large bowl and beat together with a hand-held electric whisk until pale and creamy. Fold in 75 g (3 oz) plain dark chocolate chips. Spoon the mixture into a 12-hole nonstick muffin tin lined with paper cupcake cases and bake in a preheated oven, 200°C (400°F), Gas Mark 6, for 12–14 minutes until risen and golden. Transfer to a wire rack to cool slightly, then serve warm.

CAK-MUFF-BOI

1 🕙 Lime and Coconut Snowballs

Makes 12

12 shop-bought vanilla or lemon
   cupcakes
1½ tablespoons shredded coconut

For the frosting

250 g (8 oz) cream cheese
50 g (2 oz) unsalted butter,
   softened
150 g (5 oz) icing sugar, sifted
2 teaspoons finely grated lime
   rind, plus extra thin strips to
   decorate (optional)
2 teaspoons lime juice
1½ tablespoons shredded coconut

- To make the frosting, place the cream cheese, butter, icing sugar, lime rind and juice in a large bowl and beat together with a hand-held electric whisk until very smooth, then beat in the shredded coconut.

- Spoon the frosting into a piping bag fitted with a plain nozzle, then pipe a swirl on each cupcake.

- Sprinkle with the remaining coconut and serve decorated with extra lime rind, if liked.

---

2 🕙 Lime and Coconut Cupcakes

Mix together 175 g (6 oz) sifted self-raising flour, 125 g (4 oz) caster sugar, 50 g (2 oz) desiccated coconut and a pinch of salt in a large bowl, then make a well in the centre. Add 125 ml (4 fl oz) coconut milk, 125 ml (4 fl oz) vegetable oil and 2 large lightly beaten eggs and beat well until smooth. Pour into a 12-hole muffin tin lined with paper cupcake cases and bake in a preheated oven, 200°C (400°F), Gas Mark 6, for 12–14 minutes, or until risen and firm to the touch. Meanwhile, mix together 2 tablespoons lime juice and 75 g (3 oz) sifted icing sugar, then drizzle over the warm cupcakes.

3 🕙 Lime and Coconut Whoopie Pies

Place 50 g (2 oz) softened unsalted butter, 100 g (3½ oz) caster sugar and 1 teaspoon finely grated lime rind in a bowl and beat together with a hand-held electric whisk until light and fluffy. Add 1 large egg yolk, 100 ml (3½ fl oz) coconut milk, 1 tablespoon lime juice and 25 g (1 oz) desiccated coconut and beat well. Sift in 125 g (4 oz) self-raising flour, then beat in. Pipe or drop into a greased 24-hole whoopie pie tin, or pipe or drop 24 rounds, 4–5 cm (1½–2 inches) in diameter and well spaced apart, on to 2–3 baking sheets lined with nonstick baking paper. Bake in a preheated oven, 200°C (400°F), Gas Mark 6, for 8–10 minutes until pale golden and firm to the touch. Transfer to wire racks to cool completely. Meanwhile, make a half-quantity of the frosting as above. Spread over the flat sides of half the whoopies, then sandwich together with a second biscuit.

3 Frosted Chocolate Whoopies

Makes 12–14

150 g (5 oz) self-raising flour
¼ teaspoon bicarbonate of soda
25 g (1 oz) cocoa powder
100 g (3½ oz) golden caster sugar
2 tablespoons vanilla sugar
1 egg
3 tablespoons vegetable oil
1 tablespoon milk

For the filling

125 g (4 oz) cream cheese
50 ml (2 fl oz) double cream
25 g (1 oz) vanilla sugar
50 g (2 oz) chocolate cream
  cookies, such as chocolate
  bourbons, crushed

- Line 2 baking sheets with nonstick baking paper. Place the flour, bicarbonate of soda, cocoa powder and sugars in a large bowl. Place the egg, oil and milk in another bowl and beat with a hand-held electric whisk, then add to the dry ingredients. Beat together to form a thick paste, adding a little more milk if necessary.

- Use lightly floured hands to roll the mixture into about 24 cherry-sized balls, then place well spaced apart on the prepared baking sheets.

- Bake in a preheated oven, 200°C (400°F), Gas Mark 6, for 12 minutes, or until the mixture has spread and is firm to the touch. Transfer to wire racks to cool.

- Meanwhile, make the filling. Beat together the cream cheese, cream and vanilla sugar in a large bowl until soft and creamy, then fold in the crushed cookies.

- Spread the filling mixture over the flat sides of half of the whoopies. Top each with a second biscuit and sandwich together.

---

1 Cookie Cream Bites Place 75 g (3 oz) softened unsalted butter, 125 g (4 oz) sifted icing sugar and 1 tablespoon sweetened condensed milk in a bowl and beat together until light and creamy. Stir in 50 g (2 oz) crushed chocolate cream cookies and 50 g (2 oz) finely chopped milk chocolate, then spread over 18 shop-bought chocolate mini muffins.

2 Cookie Cream Cupcakes Place 15 g (½ oz) cocoa powder in a small bowl and stir in 2 tablespoons boiling water until smooth, then stir in 50 g (2 oz) sweetened condensed milk. Place 100 g (3½ oz) softened unsalted butter, 125 g (4 oz) caster sugar, 125 g (4 oz) sifted self-raising flour, 1 teaspoon baking powder and 2 large lightly beaten eggs in a large bowl and beat together with a hand-held electric whisk until pale and creamy. Beat in the chocolate paste, then fold in 50 g (2 oz) crumbled chocolate cream cookies. Spoon the mixture into a 12-hole nonstick muffin tin lined with paper cupcake cases and bake in a preheated oven, 200°C (400°F), Gas Mark 6, for 12–14 minutes until risen and firm.

CAK-MUFF-QIM

 # Triple Chocolate Fudge Cupcakes

Makes 12

125 g (4 oz) unsalted butter, softened

125 g (4 oz) caster sugar

2 large eggs, lightly beaten

2 tablespoons chocolate hazelnut spread

125 g (4 oz) self-raising flour, sifted

1 teaspoon baking powder

25 g (1 oz) cocoa powder, sifted, pluse extra to serve

3 tablespoons mascarpone cheese

75 g (3 oz) white chocolate chunks or chips

50 g (2 oz) milk chocolate chunks or chips

crème fraîche, to serve

- Line a 12-hole nonstick muffin tin with paper cupcake cases. Place all of the ingredients except the chocolate chunks in a large bowl and beat together with a hand-held electric whisk until creamy, then fold in the chocolate chunks.

- Spoon the mixture into the prepared muffin tin and bake in a preheated oven, 200°C (400°F), Gas Mark 6, for 15 minutes, or until risen and just firm. Transfer to wire racks to cool slightly.

- Serve warm with crème fraîche, dusted with cocoa powder.

 ### Chocolate Ganache Macaroons

Place 75 g (3 oz) plain dark chocolate in a food processor and blitz until finely chopped, then tip into a bowl. Heat 50 ml (2 fl oz) double cream in a small saucepan until almost boiling, then pour over the chocolate and stir until melted and glossy. Leave to cool. Beat 50 g (2 oz) mascarpone into the cooled chocolate, then spread over 18 chocolate macaroons or soft amaretti biscuits. Sandwich each together with a second biscuit. Serve dusted with icing sugar.

 ### Double Chocolate Muffins

Sift 200 g (7 oz) plain flour, 25 g (1 oz) cocoa powder, 2 teaspoons baking powder and a pinch of salt into a large bowl, then stir in 125 g (4 oz) caster sugar. Beat together 2 large lightly beaten eggs, 100 g (3½ oz) mascarpone cheese, 50 g (2 oz) melted unsalted butter, 150 ml (¼ pint) milk and 1 teaspoon vanilla bean paste or extract in a bowl or jug. Pour into the dry ingredients, add 100 g (3½ oz) white chocolate chips or chunks and stir until just combined. Spoon the mixture into a greased or muffin case-lined 12-hole nonstick muffin tin and bake in a preheated oven, 180°C (350°F), Gas Mark 4, for 18–22 minutes until risen and firm to the touch. Serve warm.

 Shimmery Cupcakes

Makes 12

12 shop-bought strawberry
  cupcakes

For the icing

175 g (6 oz) unsalted butter,
  softened
300 g (10 oz) strawberry-
  flavoured icing sugar, sifted, or
  icing sugar mixed with 1 drop of
  red colouring
1–2 teaspoons milk or water

To decorate

edible shimmer sugar or glitter
edible sprinkles

- To make the icing, place the butter and icing sugar in a large bowl and beat together with a hand-held electric whisk, adding enough of the milk or water to form a smooth paste.

- Spoon the icing into a piping bag fitted with a star-shaped nozzle, then pipe swirls on top of the cupcakes.

- Sprinkle the cupcakes with edible sprinkles and edible shimmer sugar or glitter (make sure the glitter is clearly marked as being safe to eat).

 Fruity Cupcake Shimmers

Beat together 150 g (5 oz) sifted self-raising flour, 125 g (4 oz) softened unsalted butter, 125 g (4 oz) caster sugar, 1 teaspoon baking powder, 2 large eggs and 1 teaspoon vanilla extract until pale and creamy. Fold in 100 g (3½ oz) mixed forest fruits. Spoon into a 12-hole muffin tin lined with paper cases and bake in a preheated oven, 200°C (400°F), Gas Mark 6, for 12–14 minutes. Meanwhile, mix together 150 g (5 oz) icing sugar and 2 teaspoons cranberry juice, then drizzle over the warm cupcakes. Serve decorated as above.

 Shimmery Candy Cupcakes

Place 125 g (4 oz) each of caster sugar, softened unsalted butter and sifted self-raising flour, 1 teaspoon baking powder, 2 large lightly beaten eggs and 1 teaspoon vanilla extract in a large bowl and beat together with a hand-held electric whisk until pale and creamy. Add a few drops of red or other food colouring, then beat in until evenly coloured. Spoon the mixture into a 12-hole nonstick muffin tin lined with paper cupcake cases and bake in a preheated oven, 200°C (400°F), Gas Mark 6, for 12–14 minutes

until risen and firm to the touch. Transfer to a wire rack to cool. Meanwhile, make the icing as above and pipe swirls on the cupcakes. Decorate with sweets, such as lollipops, dolly mixtures and jelly beans, and edible sprinkles and shimmer sugar

Espresso Cup Cupcakes

Serves 4

75 g (3 oz) unsalted butter, plus extra for greasing

75 g (3 oz) plain dark chocolate, broken into small pieces

2 teaspoons coffee essence

cocoa powder, for dusting

1 large egg, lightly beaten

75 g (3 oz) soft light brown sugar

50 g (2 oz) self-raising flour

pinch of salt

To serve

crème fraîche

chocolate-covered coffee beans

- Place the butter, chocolate and coffee essence in a saucepan over a low heat and warm until just melted.

- Meanwhile, grease 4 large, ovenproof espresso cups or 175 ml (6 fl oz) ramekins with butter and dust with cocoa powder, tapping to remove any excess. Place on a baking sheet.

- Beat together the egg, sugar, flour, salt and melted chocolate in a large bowl until just combined.

- Spoon the mixture into the prepared dishes and bake in a preheated oven, 200°C (400°F), Gas Mark 6, for about 10–12 minutes until risen, but still slightly soft in the centres.

- Serve with dollops of crème fraîche and decorated with chocolate-covered coffee beans.

 Cappuccino Cream Cupcakes

Beat together 200 g (7 oz) mascarpone cheese, 125 g (4 oz) sifted icing sugar and 1 teaspoon coffee essence in a large bowl until light and creamy. Spoon the mixture into a piping bag fitted with a plain nozzle, then pipe swirls on top of 12 shop-bought coffee or chocolate cupcakes. Serve decorated with chocolate-covered coffee beans and dusted with cocoa powder.

 Hazelnut Mocha Cupcakes

Heat 200 ml (7 fl oz) double cream in a small saucepan until almost boiling, then pour over 300 g (10 oz) finely chopped or grated plain dark chocolate in a heatproof bowl and stir until melted. Leave to cool. Meanwhile, place 2 large lightly beaten eggs, 2 teaspoons coffee essence, 125 g (4 oz) caster sugar, 50 g (2 oz) sifted self-raising flour, 50 g (2 oz) ground hazelnuts and 1 teaspoon baking powder in a bowl and beat together with a hand-held electric whisk, then fold in half of the chocolate mixture. Spoon the mixture into a 12-hole nonstick muffin tin lined with paper cupcake cases and bake in a preheated oven, 200°C (400°F), Gas Mark 6, for 12–14 minutes until risen and firm to the touch. Transfer to a wire rack to cool slightly. Meanwhile, beat 150 g (5 oz) mascarpone cheese in a bowl until slightly softened, then stir in the remaining chocolate mixture. Pipe or spread over the cupcakes and decorate with chocolate-covered coffee beans.

CAK-MUFF-ZAE

QuickCook

Cakes and Traybakes

Recipes listed by cooking time

30

20

10

Salted Caramel Crunch Brownies

Makes 12–16

150 g (5 oz) unsalted butter, plus extra for greasing

150 g (5 oz) plain dark chocolate, broken into small pieces

100 g (3½ oz) dulce de leche or thick caramel sauce

2 large eggs

75 g (3 oz) soft dark brown sugar

75 g (3 oz) caster sugar

¼ teaspoon salt

50 g (2 oz) self-raising flour

100 g (3½ oz) walnut pieces, chopped

1 teaspoon sea salt flakes

- Grease a 30 x 20 cm (12 x 8 inch) brownie tin and line with nonstick baking paper (see page 9). Place the butter and chocolate in a small saucepan over a low heat and warm until just melted. In a separate saucepan, gently warm through the dulce de leche or caramel sauce.

- Meanwhile, place the eggs, brown sugar, caster sugar and salt in a large bowl and whisk until combined. Using a rubber spatula, stir in the melted chocolate, flour and half of the chopped walnut pieces.

- Scrape the mixture into the prepared tin. Scatter over the remaining walnuts, then drizzle with the dulce de leche or caramel sauce and sprinkle with the sea salt flakes.

- Bake in a preheated oven, 200°C (400°F), Gas Mark 6, for 15–18 minutes until just firm to the touch, but with a slightly fudgy texture.

- Leave to cool in the tin for 1–2 minutes, then lift on to a board using the lining paper and cut into 12–16 squares. Serve warm or cold.

 ### Salted Caramel Drizzle Brownies

Place 50 g (2 oz) blanched, unsalted peanuts in a dry frying pan and toast over a medium-low heat, shaking frequently, until golden. Leave to cool slightly on a plate. Gently warm 100 g (3½ oz) dulce de leche in a small saucepan, then stir in 1 teaspoon sea salt flakes. Scatter the peanuts over 4–6 warmed shop-bought brownies, then drizzle with the caramel sauce. Serve with vanilla ice cream.

Caramel Brownie Cookies

Place 75 g (3 oz) unsalted butter, 75 g (3 oz) plain dark chocolate, broken into small pieces, and 1 tablespoon dulce de leche or thick caramel sauce in a small saucepan over a low heat and warm until just melted. Meanwhile, place 1 large egg, 100 g (3½ oz) soft dark brown sugar and ¼ teaspoon salt in a large bowl and whisk until combined. Using a rubber spatula, stir in the melted chocolate and 100 g (3½ oz) self-raising flour. Drop 14–18 dessertspoonfuls of the mixture, well spaced apart, on to 2 baking sheets lined with nonstick baking paper. Bake in a preheated oven, 180°C (350°F), Gas Mark 4, for 8 minutes, or until just firm to the touch. Transfer to wire racks using a palette knife. Serve warm or cold.

White Chocolate and Raspberry Trifle Slices

Serves 6

100 g (3½ oz) white chocolate, broken into small pieces

75 ml (3 fl oz) sweet sherry

1 shop-bought Madeira loaf cake, about 300 g (10 oz), cut into 6 slices

200 g (7 oz) mascarpone cheese

125 ml (4 fl oz) double cream

1 tablespoon vanilla sugar

150 ml (¼ pint) shop-bought fresh thick custard

300 g (10 oz) raspberries

white chocolate curls or shavings, to decorate

- Melt the chocolate in a heatproof bowl set over a saucepan of gently simmering water, ensuring the bowl does not touch the water, then leave to cool.

- Meanwhile, pour the sherry into a shallow bowl and dip in each of the cake slices to just dampen. Place in 6 serving dishes and set aside.

- Place the mascarpone, cream and vanilla sugar in a large bowl and beat with a hand-held electric whisk until thick. Fold in the cooled chocolate and custard.

- Scatter half of the raspberries over the soaked cake slices, then spoon over the custard cream.

- Scatter with the remaining raspberries and serve decorated with white chocolate curls or shavings.

2 **White Choc and Raspberry Trifle**

Gently heat 300 g (10 oz) raspberries, 2 tablespoons icing sugar and 2 tablespoons crème de cassis until the fruit is just collapsing. Meanwhile, place 150 g (5 oz) shop-bought Madeira loaf cake, cut into cubes, in a bowl. Pour over the berries, then cover and chill for 10–12 minutes. Meanwhile, whip 150 ml (¼ pint) double cream and 1 teaspoon vanilla bean paste until it forms soft peaks, then fold in 50 g (2 oz) finely grated white chocolate. Spoon 250 g (8 oz) thick raspberry yogurt and 125 g (4 oz) raspberries over the sponge, then top with the whipped cream.

3 **White Choc and Raspberry**

Traybake Place 125 g (4 oz) softened unsalted butter, 125 g (4 oz) caster sugar, 100 g (3½ oz) ground almonds, 75 g (3 oz) sifted self-raising flour, 1 teaspoon baking powder, 2 large lightly beaten eggs, 1–2 tablespoons milk and 1 teaspoon almond extract in a large bowl and beat together with a hand-held electric whisk until pale and creamy. Spoon into a greased 34 x 20 cm (13½ x 8 inch) brownie tin lined with nonstick baking paper and scatter over 75 g (3 oz) white chocolate chunks and 50 g (2 oz) crumbled, frozen raspberries.

Bake in a preheated oven, 200°C (400°F), Gas Mark 6, for 20 minutes, or until risen and golden. Turn out of the tin on to a wire rack and peel away the lining paper. Serve warm or cold, cut into 12–16 squares. Bake in a preheated oven, 200°C (400°F), Gas Mark 6, for 20 minutes, or until risen and golden. Turn out of the tin on to a wire rack and peel away the lining paper. Serve warm or cold, cut into 12–16 squares.

30 Crunchy Pineapple and Treacle Rockcakes

Makes 10–12

250 g (8 oz) self-raising flour
1½ teaspoons baking powder
125 g (4 oz) unsalted butter,
   softened
100 g (3½ oz) demerara sugar
2 teaspoons grated orange rind
50 g (2 oz) desiccated coconut
100 g (3½ oz) canned pineapple
   in juice, drained and chopped
1 large egg, lightly beaten
50 g (2 oz) black treacle
1–2 tablespoons pineapple juice

For the topping

3 tablespoons chopped almonds
2 tablespoons demerara sugar

- Line 2 baking sheets with nonstick baking paper. Sift the flour and baking powder into a large bowl. Add the butter and rub in with the fingertips until the mixture resembles fine breadcrumbs, then stir in the sugar, orange rind, coconut and pineapple.

- Mix together the egg and treacle in a small jug. Pour into the dry ingredients and mix to combine, adding enough of the pineapple juice to form a stiff, sticky mixture.

- Drop 10–12 rough-surfaced mounds of the mixture on to the prepared baking sheets. Mix together the topping ingredients in a small bowl, then sprinkle over each mound.

- Bake in a preheated oven, 200°C (400°F), Gas Mark 6, for 18–20 minutes until golden. Transfer to wire racks to cool slightly, then serve warm.

10 Crunchy Pineapple Trifles

Gently fry 50 g (2 oz) rolled oats, 25 g (1 oz) desiccated coconut and 25 g (1 oz) demerara sugar in 25 g (1 oz) butter for 3–4 minutes, stirring frequently. Leave to cool on kitchen paper. Meanwhile, sandwich together 20 soft amaretti biscuits with 2–3 tablespoons apricot jam, then cut each one in half and place in 4 serving dishes. Drizzle each with 2 teaspoons rum and divide 150 g (5 oz) sliced pineapple over the bases. Pour 3 tablespoons shop-bought fresh custard over each trifle, then top with whipped cream and the crunchy topping.

20 Tropical Treacle Chews

Beat together 150 g (5 oz) softened unsalted butter, 1 teaspoon grated orange rind, 150 g (5 oz) golden caster sugar, 1 tablespoon black treacle and 1 large beaten egg in a large bowl. Stir in 75 g (3 oz) mixed ready-to-eat semi-dried tropical fruits, chopped, 25 g (1 oz) desiccated coconut, 225 g (7½ oz) plain flour and ½ teaspoon bicarbonate of soda. Roll the mixture into about 24 walnut-sized balls and place, well spaced apart, on 2 baking sheets lined with nonstick baking paper, then flatten slightly. Mix 2 tablespoons desiccated coconut and 1 tablespoon demerara or granulated sugar in a small bowl, then sprinkle the topping over the cookies. Bake in a preheated oven, 200°C (400°F), Gas Mark 6, for 10 minutes, or until golden but still slightly soft. Leave to cool on the baking sheets for 1 minute, then transfer to wire racks to cool completely.

3 Chocolate Berry Roulade

Serves 6

125 g (4 oz) plain dark chocolate,
   broken into small pieces
butter, for greasing
4 large eggs, separated
125 g (4 oz) caster sugar
200 g (7 oz) mascarpone cheese
150 g (5 oz) crème fraîche
seeds scraped from 1 vanilla pod
   or 1 teaspoon vanilla bean paste
250 g (8 oz) mixed summer
   berries, thawed if frozen
icing sugar, for dusting

• Melt the chocolate in a heatproof bowl over a saucepan of gently simmering water, ensuring the bowl does not touch the water, then leave to cool.

• Meanwhile, grease a 23 x 33 (9 x 13 inch) Swiss roll tin and line with nonstick baking paper. In a large bowl, beat the egg yolks and sugar with a hand-held electric whisk until pale and thick. Whisk the egg whites in a clean bowl until stiff. Fold the cooled chocolate into the egg yolk mixture, then the egg whites.

• Pour the mixture into the tin and bake in a preheated oven, 200°C (400°F), Gas Mark 6, for 12–14 minutes until slightly springy to the touch. Cover with a piece of baking paper, lay a large board on top and invert the sponge on to the board. Remove the baking paper, trim the edges and leave to cool for 5–6 minutes.

• Meanwhile, beat together the mascarpone, crème fraîche and vanilla in a bowl until thickened. Spread over the roulade and scatter with half the berries. Using the baking paper, roll up the sponge lengthways, then dust with icing sugar. Decorate with the remaining berries.

---

1 **Berry Sponges with Chocolate Sauce**

Melt 200 g (7 oz) plain dark chocolate and 200 ml (7 fl oz) double cream in a bowl over a saucepan of simmering water. Meanwhile, cut 1 shop-bought chocolate roulade into 6 slices. Divide 300 g (10 oz) mixed summer berries over the slices and drizzle the chocolate sauce over the top.

2 **Chocolate Fondants with Berry Sauce** Gently melt 125 g (4 oz) butter and 150 g (5 oz) plain dark chocolate in a saucepan. Beat 2 large eggs, 2 large egg yolks and 50 g (2 oz) soft light brown sugar until thick and creamy. Fold in 25 g (1 oz) plain flour and the chocolate. Spoon the mixture into 6 greased and floured ramekins,

and push a chunk of white chocolate into each. Place on a baking sheet and bake in a preheated oven, 200°C (400°F), Gas Mark 6, for 10–12 minutes until risen but still with a slight wobble. Cool the fondants in the dishes for 1–2 minutes, then invert on to 6 serving dishes. Serve with warm ready-made red fruit coulis.

 # Mint and Chocolate Fudge Brownie Sundaes

Serves 4

2 or 3 shop-bought chocolate
  fudge brownies, cubed
4 scoops of mint ice cream
4 scoops of chocolate ice cream
aerosol can of whipped cream
2 tablespoons pistachio nut
  kernels, roughly chopped

For the fudge sauce

125 g (4 oz) plain dark chocolate,
  broken into small pieces
25 g (1 oz) unsalted butter
1 tablespoon golden syrup
1 teaspoon peppermint extract
75 ml (3 fl oz) double cream

- To make the fudge sauce, place all the ingredients in a small saucepan over a low heat and warm until the chocolate has melted. Scrape into a bowl and leave to cool for 2–3 minutes.

- Stir the fudge sauce until glossy, then spoon 1 tablespoon into each of 4 tall sundae glasses.

- Drop the cubed brownies into the glasses, then top each sundae with 1 scoop of mint ice cream and 1 scoop of chocolate ice cream.

- Drizzle another 1 tablespoon of the fudge sauce over each, then generously swirl the whipped cream over the sauce. Serve scattered with the pistachios.

 Mint Caramel Drizzle Brownies

Place 200 g (7 oz) dulce de leche or thick caramel sauce, 1 teaspoon peppermint extract and 75 g (3 oz) mint-flavoured or plain dark chocolate, broken into pieces, into a small saucepan over a low heat and warm until the chocolate has melted. Put 4 warmed shop-bought chocolate brownies in 4 serving dishes and top each with 1 scoop of mint choc chip or pistachio ice cream. Drizzle over the sauce and scatter over 50 g (2 oz) pistachio nuts. Serve immediately, decorated with mint leaves.

 Peppermint and Pistachio Brownies

Place 150 g (5 oz) unsalted butter and 200 g (7 oz) mint-flavoured plain dark chocolate, broken into small pieces, in a small saucepan over a low heat and warm until just melted. Meanwhile, place 2 large eggs, 150 g (5 oz) soft dark brown sugar and ½ teaspoon peppermint extract in a bowl and whisk until combined. Using a rubber spatula, stir in the melted chocolate, 50 g (2 oz) self-raising flour, 50 g (2 oz) roughly chopped pistachio nuts and 75 g (3 oz) white chocolate chunks. Scrape the mixture into a

greased 23 cm (9 inch) square brownie tin lined with nonstick baking paper (see page 9) and bake in a preheated oven, 200°C (400°F), Gas Mark 6, for 15–18 minutes until slightly risen and not quite firm. Leave to cool in the tin for 1–2 minutes, then lift on to a board using the lining paper and cut into 12–16 squares. Serve warm or cold.

30 Prune and Apple Wedges

Makes 8

75 g (3 oz) ready-to-eat semi-dried prunes, chopped

75 g (3 oz) shop-bought apple purée

1 tablespoon runny honey, plus extra to serve

about 50 ml (2 fl oz) apple juice, plus extra for brushing

250 g (8 oz) plain flour, plus extra for dusting

¼ teaspoon salt

1 teaspoon bicarbonate of soda

2 teaspoons cream of tartar

½ teaspoon mixed spice

50 g (2 oz) unsalted butter, softened

1 large egg, lightly beaten

Greek yogurt and honey, to serve

- Line a large baking sheet with nonstick baking paper. Place the prunes, apple purée, honey and apple juice in a bowl. Stir together, then set aside.

- Sift the flour, salt, bicarbonate of soda, cream of tartar and mixed spice into a large bowl. Add the butter and rub in with the fingertips until the mixture resembles fine breadcrumbs. Make a well in the centre and pour in the egg. Add the prune and apple mixture and mix to form a soft but not sticky dough, adding a little extra apple juice if necessary.

- Turn the dough out on to a floured surface and shape into a 20 cm (8 inch) circle, then cut into 8 wedges. Place on the prepared baking sheet and brush with extra apple juice.

- Bake in a preheated oven, 220°C (425°F), Gas Mark 7, for 12 minutes, or until risen and golden. Transfer to a wire rack to cool slightly, then serve warm with Greek yogurt and honey.

---

1 **Apple Pancakes**

Sift together 150 g (5 oz) self-raising flour, 1 teaspoon baking powder and ½ teaspoon mixed spice, then stir in 1 small grated apple and 2 tablespoons caster sugar. Whisk in 1 large beaten egg, 50 g (2 oz) shop-bought apple purée, 1 tablespoon runny honey and 175 ml (6 fl oz) milk. Heat a small knob of butter in a large frying pan, add spoonfuls of batter and cook for 1–2 minutes, flip and cook for a further 30–60 seconds. Repeat to make 16–18 pancakes. Drizzle with honey and serve with chopped prunes.

2 **Prune and Apple Scones**

Place 50 g (2 oz) cold, diced unsalted butter, 225 g (7½ oz) self-raising flour and 2 teaspoons baking powder in a food processor and pulse until the mixture resembles fine breadcrumbs. Add 75 g (3 oz) ready-to-eat semi-dried chopped prunes, 1 small peeled, cored and grated dessert apple, 25 g (1 oz) caster sugar, ¼ teaspoon salt and ½ teaspoon mixed spice and pulse briefly to mix, then add 1 large lightly beaten egg and 75 g (3 oz) shop-bought apple purée. Pulse again, adding enough of 2–3 tablespoons apple juice to form a soft but not sticky dough. Roll out on a floured surface, then stamp out 10 rounds using a 6 cm (2½ inch) fluted cutter, without twisting the cutter. Place on 2 baking sheets lined with nonstick baking paper and bake in a preheated oven, 220°C (425°F), Gas Mark 7, for 10–12 minutes until risen and golden. Serve warm with Greek yogurt and honey.

CAK-CAKE-KAP

30 Lemon Cheesecake Blondies

Makes 12–16

125 g (4 oz) unsalted butter, plus
extra for greasing
100 g (3½ oz) white chocolate,
broken into small pieces
50 g (2 oz) cream cheese
2 large eggs
100 g (3½ oz) soft light
brown sugar
1 teaspoon lemon extract
¼ teaspoon salt
150 g (5 oz) plain flour
raspberry coulis, to serve
(optional)

For the topping

125 g (4 oz) cream cheese
1 large egg yolk
50 g (2 oz) caster sugar
1 teaspoon finely grated
lemon rind

- Grease a 23 cm (9 inch) square brownie tin and line with nonstick baking paper (see page 9). Place the butter and white chocolate in a small saucepan over a low heat and warm until just melted.

- Meanwhile, make the topping. Beat together all the ingredients in a small bowl until smooth.

- Place the cream cheese, eggs, brown sugar, lemon extract and salt in a large bowl and beat together until smooth. Using a rubber spatula, stir in the melted chocolate and flour.

- Scrape the mixture into the prepared tin. Spoon over the topping and swirl the two mixtures together with the tip of a knife.

- Bake in a preheated oven, 200°C (400°F), Gas Mark 6, for 15–17 minutes until golden.

- Leave to cool in the tin for 1–2 minutes, then lift on to a board using the lining paper and cut into 12–16 squares. Serve warm or cold with raspberry coulis, if liked.

 Quick Lemon Cream Layer Cake

Slice a 20 cm (8 inch) shop-bought lemon or vanilla sponge cake in half horizontally and spread the cut side of the base with 4 tablespoons lemon curd. Place 75 g (3 oz) cream cheese, 150 ml (¼ pint) double cream, 1 teaspoon finely grated lemon rind and 50 g (2 oz) vanilla sugar in a large bowl and beat with a hand-held electric whisk until light and creamy, then spoon over the lemon curd. Replace the top half of the cake and sandwich together. Serve dusted with icing sugar.

 Lemon Cheesecake Slices

Beat together 125 g (4 oz) cream cheese, 50 g (2 oz) caster sugar, 1 teaspoon finely grated lemon rind and 100 g (3½ oz) crème fraiche in a large bowl until smooth. Fold in 50 g (2 oz) white chocolate chips. Spread the topping thickly over 4 shop-bought blondies or chocolate brownies. Scatter over 125 g (4 oz) raspberries and serve dusted with icing sugar.

CAK-CAKE-GOD

Rocky Road Brownie Bites

Makes 24

150 g (5 oz) milk chocolate, broken into small pieces

25 g (1 oz) unsalted butter

6 shop-bought chocolate brownies, cut into quarters

75 g (3 oz) shortbread fingers, roughly chopped or broken

50 g (2 oz) glacé cherries, quartered

50 g (2 oz) whole toasted hazelnuts

25 g (1 oz) mini marshmallows

- Melt the chocolate and butter in a heatproof bowl set over a saucepan of gently simmering water, ensuring the bowl does not touch the water, until just melted but not hot.

- Meanwhile, line a baking sheet with nonstick baking paper and place the brownies on to the sheet.

- Place the remaining ingredients in a large bowl, then pour over the melted chocolate and stir until all the ingredients are well coated.

- Spoon the mixture on to the brownies, then chill in the freezer for 8–10 minutes until the chocolate has set.

 Rocky Road Brownie Layers

Gently warm through 125 ml (4 fl oz) shop-bought Belgian chocolate sauce in a saucepan. Cut 4 shop-bought chocolate brownies into cubes and arrange in the bottom of 6 serving dishes. Top each with 1 scoop of chocolate ice cream, then scatter over 25 g (1 oz) mini marshmallows. Drizzle the warmed chocolate sauce over the marshmallows and scatter over 25 g (1 oz) chopped toasted hazelnuts. Serve immediately.

 Rocky Road Brownies

Warm 150 g (5 oz) unsalted butter and 75 g (3 oz) each of plain dark and milk chocolate, broken into small pieces, in a small saucepan over a low heat until just melted. Meanwhile, place 2 large eggs, 125 g (4 oz) caster sugar and a pinch of salt in a bowl and whisk until combined. Using a rubber spatula, stir in the melted chocolate, 50 g (2 oz) chopped toasted hazelnuts, 75 g (3 oz) halved glacé cherries and 50 g (2 oz) self-raising flour. Scrape the mixture into a greased 30 x 20 cm (12 x 8 inch) brownie tin lined with nonstick baking paper (see page 9) and bake in a preheated oven, 200 °C (400 °F), Gas Mark 6, for 15 minutes until just firm to the touch, but with a slightly fudgy texture. Remove from the oven and scatter with 25 g (1 oz) mini marshmallows, then return to the oven for a further 1–2 minutes until the marshmallows are just pale golden. Leave to cool in the tin for 2–3 minutes, then lift on to a board using the lining paper and cut into 12–16 squares. Serve warm or cold.

30 Traditional Fruity Rockcakes

Makes 10–12

250 g (8 oz) self-raising flour
1½ teaspoons baking powder
1 teaspoon ground cinnamon
½ teaspoon ground ginger
125 g (4 oz) unsalted butter,
    softened
100 g (3½ oz) demerara sugar,
    plus extra for sprinkling
    (optional)
1 teaspoon grated orange rind
100 g (3½ oz) sultanas
75 g (3 oz) currants
50 g (2 oz) mixed peel or
    chopped glacé cherries
1 large egg, lightly beaten
3–4 tablespoons milk

· Line a large baking sheet with nonstick baking paper. Sift the flour, baking powder and spices into a large bowl. Add the butter and rub in with the fingertips until the mixture resembles fine breadcrumbs, then stir in the sugar, orange rind, sultanas, currants and mixed peel or cherries. Pour in the egg, adding enough of the milk to form a soft, slightly sticky dough.

· Drop 10–12 mounds of the mixture on to the prepared baking sheet so that they resemble rocks and sprinkle with a little extra sugar, if using.

· Bake in a preheated oven, 200°C (400°F), Gas Mark 6, for 18–20 minutes until golden. Transfer to a wire rack to cool slightly, then serve warm.

 Quick Fruity Scones

Place 1 teaspoon grated orange rind, 100 g (3½ oz) sultanas, 75 g (3 oz) currants, 50 g (2 oz) mixed peel or chopped glacé cherries, 1½ teaspoons mixed spice and 150 g (5 oz) slightly softened unsalted butter in a food processor and blend until smooth, then scrape on to a sheet of clingfilm or greaseproof paper. Roll the butter into a sausage shape and chill until needed. To serve, split 12–14 warmed shop-bought scones in half and spread with the fruity spiced butter.

 Mini Fruity Rockcakes

Sift 250 g (8 oz) self-raising flour, 1½ teaspoons baking powder, 1 teaspoon ground cinnamon and ½ teaspoon ground ginger into a food processor and add 125 g (4 oz) cold, diced unsalted butter. Pulse until the mixture resembles fine breadcrumbs, then stir in 1 peeled and grated dessert apple and 75 g (3 oz) sultanas or finely chopped dates. Add 1 large beaten egg and a little milk, if necessary, and mix to form a soft, slightly sticky dough. Drop 18–20 small spoonfuls of the mixture on to 2 baking sheets lined with nonstick baking paper. Bake in a preheated oven, 200°C (400°F), Gas Mark 6, for 10–12 minutes until golden. Transfer to wire racks to cool.

CAK-CAKE-COP

10 Swiss Roll Baked Alaskas

Serves 4

3 large egg whites
150 g (5 oz) caster sugar
1 shop-bought strawberry and
vanilla jumbo Swiss roll, cut into
8 x 1.5 cm (¾ inch) slices
4 scoops of vanilla, strawberry or
raspberry ripple ice cream

- Line a baking sheet with nonstick baking paper and chill in the freezer. Meanwhile, whisk the egg whites in a clean bowl with a hand-held electric whisk until stiff, then gradually whisk in the sugar, beating well between each addition, until the mixture is thick and glossy.

- Arrange 4 slices of Swiss roll, well spaced apart, on the prepared baking sheet. Top each one with 1 scoop of the frozen ice cream, then top with the remaining slices of Swiss roll. Spoon the meringue mixture over each one, ensuring that the ice cream and sponge is completely covered.

- Bake in a preheated oven, 200°C (400°F), Gas Mark 6, for 3–4 minutes until the meringue is lightly golden. Serve immediately.

2 Swiss Roll Tiramisu

Cut 1 shop-bought chocolate and vanilla Swiss roll into slices and arrange in a large glass or trifle bowl. Pour over 75 ml (3 fl oz) strong, sweetened espresso coffee and leave to soak. Meanwhile, place 4 tablespoons sifted icing sugar, 200 g (7 oz) mascarpone cheese and 150 ml (¼ pint) double cream in a bowl and beat together with a hand-held electric whisk until thick and smooth. Spoon over the Swiss roll and chill for 10–15 minutes. Serve decorated with chocolate curls.

3 Classic Swiss Roll

Place 3 large eggs, 100 g (3½ oz) caster sugar and 1 teaspoon vanilla bean paste in a large bowl and beat with a hand-held electric whisk until pale and thick. Fold in 100 g (3½ oz) sifted self-raising flour, then pour into a greased 33 x 23 cm (13 x 9 inch) Swiss roll tin lined with nonstick baking paper. Bake in a preheated oven, 200°C (400°F), Gas Mark 6, for 10–12 minutes until golden and slightly springy to the touch. Meanwhile, lay a large piece of baking paper on a tea towel and sprinkle with 2 tablespoons caster sugar. Turn the sponge out on to the paper and peel away the paper from the sponge base. Trim the edges with a sharp knife and lightly score one narrow end. From the scored end, roll up the sponge quite tightly, using the tea towel to help. Gently unroll it and cool for 2–3 minutes before spreading with an even layer of 175 g (6 oz) jam. Reroll the sponge tightly and cut into slices to serve.

 # Drop Scones with Ginger Syrup

Makes 8–12

8–12 shop-bought drop scones or Scotch pancakes

4–6 scoops of vanilla ice cream, to serve (optional)

Ginger syrup

50 g (2 oz) unsalted butter

2 tablespoons golden syrup

25 g (1 oz) soft dark brown sugar

4 tablespoons double cream

½–1 teaspoon ground ginger, according to taste

15 g (½ oz) piece of stem ginger in syrup, cut into matchsticks

- To make the ginger syrup, place the ingredients in a small saucepan over a low heat and heat gently, stirring occasionally, until the sugar has dissolved.

- Meanwhile, warm the drop scones under a preheated medium grill for 1–2 minutes, turning once.

- Serve the drop scones topped with scoops of ice cream, if liked, with the ginger syrup drizzled over.

---

 2 Ginger Glazed Scones

Sift 250 g (8 oz) self-raising flour, 2 teaspoons baking powder and 1 teaspoon ground ginger into a large bowl. Add 50 g (2 oz) softened unsalted butter and rub in with the fingertips until the mixture resembles fine breadcrumbs, then stir in 2 tablespoons golden caster sugar and 2 x 15 g (½ oz) pieces of finely chopped stem ginger in syrup. Make a well in the centre and pour in 125 ml (4 fl oz) buttermilk, then mix to form a soft dough, adding a little extra buttermilk if necessary. Roll out on a floured surface to 1.5 cm (¾ inch) thick, then stamp out 10–12 rounds using a 6 cm (2½ inch) fluted cutter, without twisting the cutter. Place on 2 baking sheets lined with baking paper and bake in a preheated oven, 220°C (425°F), Gas Mark 7, for 10 minutes, or until risen and golden. Meanwhile, sift 50 g (2 oz) icing sugar and 1 teaspoon ground ginger into a small bowl. Stir in 1 tablespoon melted unsalted butter and a splash of milk, if necessary, and mix until smooth. Drizzle the scones with the gingery glaze. Serve warm.

 3 Crystallized Ginger Rockcakes

Beat together 100 g (3½ oz) softened butter and 100 g (3½ oz) caster sugar until light and fluffy. Add 1 large lightly beaten egg and beat well. Sift in 200 g (7 oz) self-raising flour, 1 teaspoon baking powder and 1 teaspoon ground ginger. Add 75 g (3 oz) dried apricots, chopped, and 50 g (2 oz) crystallized ginger, finely chopped, and mix to a soft, slightly sticky mixture, adding a little milk if necessary. Drop 8–10 mounds of the mixture on to 2 lined baking sheets and bake in a preheated oven, 200°C (400°F), Gas Mark 6, for about 15–18 minutes until golden. Transfer to a wire rack to cool.

30 Blackcurrant Sandwich Sponge

Makes 1 x 20 cm (8 inch) cake

125 g (4 oz) unsalted butter, softened, plus extra for greasing

125 g (4 oz) caster sugar, plus extra for sprinkling

125 g (4 oz) self-raising flour, sifted

1 teaspoon baking powder

1 teaspoon ground ginger

2 large eggs, lightly beaten

1 tablespoon milk

4 tablespoons blackcurrant jam

- Grease 2 x 20 cm (8 inch) round cake tins and line with nonstick baking paper.

- Place all of the ingredients except the jam in a large bowl and beat together with a hand-held electric whisk until pale and creamy.

- Divide the mixture between the prepared tins and bake in a preheated oven, 200°C (400°F), Gas Mark 6, for 15–18 minutes until risen and firm to the touch. Turn the cakes out of the tins on to wire racks, peel away the lining paper and leave to cool.

- Spread 1 cooled cake thickly with the blackcurrant jam and top with the second. Sprinkle with caster sugar and serve cut into wedges.

 Blackcurrant and Sponge Eton Mess
Cut 1 shop-bought Jamaica ginger loaf into cubes and place in a large bowl with 200 g (7 oz) blackcurrants. Beat together 250 g (8 oz) Greek yogurt, 2 tablespoon crème de cassis, ½ teaspoon ground ginger and 2 tablespoons caster sugar in a separate bowl, then fold into the sponge. Spoon into 4 serving dishes and serve immediately.

 Blackcurrant-Soaked Ginger Slices Arrange 8 slices of slightly stale shop-bought gingerbread or Jamaica ginger loaf in 4 serving dishes. Place 300 g (10 oz) fresh or frozen blackcurrants, 2 tablespoons crème de cassis, 75 g (3 oz) soft light brown sugar and 15 g (½ oz) chopped stem ginger in syrup in a saucepan and heat gently, stirring occasionally, until the sugar has dissolved and the fruit collapsed. Leave to cool for a few minutes. Spoon over the gingerbread and serve with crème fraîche or ice cream.

30 Double Fruit and Nut Brownies

Makes 12–16

150 g (5 oz) unsalted butter, plus extra for greasing

175 g (6 oz) plain dark chocolate, broken into small pieces

2 large eggs

75 g (3 oz) soft dark brown sugar

75 g (3 oz) caster sugar

½ teaspoon orange extract (optional)

25 g (1 oz) self-raising flour

pinch of salt

50 g (2 oz) ground almonds

75 g (3 oz) raisins

50 g (2 oz) dried cranberries

50 g (2 oz) Brazil nuts, chopped

- Grease a 30 x 20 cm (12 x 8 inch) brownie tin and line with nonstick baking paper (see page 9). Place the butter and chocolate in a small saucepan over a low heat and warm until just melted.

- Meanwhile, place the eggs, brown sugar and caster sugar in a large bowl and whisk until combined. Using a rubber spatula, stir in the melted chocolate and all the remaining ingredients.

- Scrape the mixture into the prepared tin and bake in a preheated oven, 200°C (400°F), Gas Mark 6, for 15–18 minutes until just firm to the touch, but with a slightly fudgy texture.

- Leave to cool in the tin for 1–2 minutes, then lift on to a board using the lining paper and cut into 12–16 squares. Serve warm or cold.

 Kitsch Fruit and Nut Brownie Sundaes Chop 4 shop-bought warmed brownies and place in the bottom of 4 serving dishes, then top each one with 1 scoop of chocolate fudge brownie or chocolate ice cream. Swirl over aerosol whipped cream and drizzle each with 1 tablespoon shop-bought strawberry or Belgian chocolate sauce. Scatter 1 teaspoon chopped toasted hazelnuts over each sundae and top with 1 glacé cherry. Serve with mini sparklers, if liked.

 Fruit and Nut Brownie Buns Place 150 g (5 oz) unsalted butter and 175 g (6 oz) plain dark chocolate, broken into small pieces, in a small saucepan over a low heat and warm until just melted. Meanwhile, place 2 large eggs, 75 g (3 oz) brown sugar and 75 g (3 oz) caster sugar in a large bowl and whisk until combined. Using a rubber spatula, stir in the melted chocolate, ½ teaspoon orange extract (optional), 25 g (1 oz) self-raising flour, a pinch of salt, 50 g (2 oz) ground almonds, 50 g (2 oz) dried cranberries and 50 g (2 oz) chopped toasted hazelnuts. Spoon the mixture into a 12-hole nonstick muffin tin lined with paper cupcake cases and bake in a preheated oven, 200°C (400°F), Gas Mark 6, for 10–12 minutes until slightly firm. Serve with single cream, if liked.

Wholemeal Sultana Pikelets

Makes 18–20

75 g (3 oz) self-raising flour
75 g (3 oz) wholemeal self-raising
flour
1 teaspoon baking powder
2 tablespoons soft light
brown sugar
1 large egg, lightly beaten
½ teaspoon vanilla bean paste or
vanilla extract
225 ml (7½ fl oz) buttermilk
50 g (2 oz) golden sultanas
1 small dessert apple, peeled,
cored and coarsely grated
(optional)
butter, for frying
warm maple syrup, to serve

- Sift the flours and baking powder into a bowl, then stir in the sugar and make a well in the centre. Whisk together the egg, vanilla paste or extract and buttermilk in a jug, then pour into the well. Whisk together, gradually incorporating the flour from the edges until the batter is smooth and thick. Stir in the golden sultanas and grated apple, if using.

- Heat a small knob of butter in each of 2 large, nonstick frying pans, add tablespoonfuls of the batter and cook for 1 minute until bubbles start to appear on the surface, then flip over and cook for a further 30–60 seconds until lightly golden. Repeat with the remaining batter to make 18–20 pikelets, adding a little more butter to the pan if necessary.

- Serve warm, drizzled with warm maple syrup.

Wholemeal Sultana Griddle Scones

Sift 100 g (3½ oz) wholemeal flour, 125 g (4 oz) plain flour, 3 teaspoons baking powder and a pinch of salt into a large bowl. Rub in 50 g (2 oz) softened butter, then stir in 2 tablespoons light soft brown sugar, 50 g (2 oz) golden sultanas and 1 teaspoon finely grated orange rind. Add enough of 125 ml (4 fl oz) milk to form a soft dough. Shape into a 20 cm (8 inch) circle, then cut into 8 wedges. Lightly grease a large, nonstick frying pan with oil, add the scones and cook over a medium heat for 5–6 minutes on each side.

Wholemeal Sultana Scones

Sift 100 g (3½ oz) wholemeal self-raising flour, 150 g (5 oz) self-raising flour and 2 teaspoons baking powder into a large bowl. Add 50 g (2 oz) softened unsalted butter and rub in with the fingertips until the mixture resembles fine breadcrumbs, then stir in 2 tablespoons soft light brown sugar, 75 g (3 oz) sultanas and 1 small dessert apple, peeled, cored and coarsely grated, if liked. Make a well in the centre and pour in 150 ml (¼ pint) buttermilk, then mix to form a soft dough. Roll out on a floured surface to 1.5 cm (¾ inch) thick, then stamp out 8–10 rounds using a 7 cm (3 inch) fluted cutter, without twisting the cutter. Place on 2 baking sheets lined with nonstick baking paper and brush with a little extra buttermilk. Bake in a preheated oven, 220°C (425°F), Gas Mark 7, for 12 minutes, or until risen and golden. Transfer to wire racks to cool slightly, then dust with icing sugar. Serve split in half with unsalted butter.

 # Chocolate Sponge Puddings with Praline Sauce

Serves 6

6 slices of shop-bought chocolate
sponge cake or 6 chocolate
brownies
6 scoops of pralines and cream
ice cream

For the praline sauce

50 g (2 oz) unsalted butter
200 ml (7 fl oz) double cream
1 tablespoon agave nectar, honey
or golden syrup
75 g (3 oz) soft dark brown sugar
100 g (3½ oz) Belgian praline
chocolates
75 g (3 oz) pecan nut halves

• Wrap the slices of sponge cake or brownies in foil and place
in a preheated oven, 180°C (350°F), Gas Mark 4, for 5–6
minutes to warm through.

• Meanwhile, make the praline sauce. Place the butter, cream,
agave nectar, honey or golden syrup and sugar in a small
saucepan and heat gently until the butter has melted and
the sugar dissolved. Add the praline chocolate and stir until
smooth, then stir in the pecans.

• Place the warmed chocolate sponge or brownies in 6 serving
dishes and top each with 1 scoop of the ice cream. Drizzle
over the warm sauce and serve immediately.

 ### Chocolate Praline Cupcakes

Place 2 tablespoons cocoa powder
in a bowl and stir in 2 tablespoons
boiling water until smooth. Add
125 g (4 oz) each of softened
unsalted butter, caster sugar and
sifted self-raising flour, 1 teaspoon
baking powder, 2 large lightly
beaten eggs and 1 tablespoon
milk and beat together until pale
and creamy. Fold in 50 g (2 oz)
finely chopped Belgian praline
chocolates and 50 g (2 oz)
chopped pecan nuts. Spoon the
mixture into a 12-hole muffin tin
lined with paper cases and bake in
a preheated oven, 200°C (400°F),
Gas Mark 6, for 12–14 minutes until
firm to the touch. Serve warm.

 ### Chocolate Praline Traybake

Place 150 g (5 oz) softened
unsalted butter, 150 g (5 oz) soft
light brown sugar, 125 g (4 oz)
sifted self-raising flour, 25 g
(1 oz) sifted good-quality cocoa
powder, 1 teaspoon baking
powder, 2 large lightly beaten
eggs, 1 teaspoon vanilla extract
and 2 tablespoons milk in a large
bowl and beat together with a
hand-held electric whisk until
pale and creamy. Fold in 100 g
(3½ oz) chopped Belgian praline
chocolates and 50 g (2 oz)
chopped pecan nuts. Spoon into
a greased 30 x 20 cm (12 x 8 inch)
brownie tin lined with nonstick
baking paper and bake in a

preheated oven, 200°C
(400°F), Gas Mark 6, for 18–20
minutes until risen and firm to
the touch. Turn out of the tin on
to a wire rack and peel away the
lining paper. Serve warm or cold,
cut into 12–16 squares.

30 ◖ Blackcurrant Swirl Blondies

Makes 12–16

175 g (6 oz) unsalted butter,
  melted, plus extra for greasing
3 large eggs
125 g (4 oz) soft light brown sugar
50 g (2 oz) caster sugar
1 teaspoon almond extract
pinch of salt
100 g (3½ oz) ground almonds
75 g (3 oz) plain flour
3 tablespoons ready-made
  blackcurrant coulis

To serve

blackcurrant sorbet
toasted flaked almonds

- Grease a 23 cm (9 inch) square brownie tin and line with nonstick baking paper (see page 9).

- Place the eggs, brown sugar and caster sugar in a large bowl and whisk until combined. Stir in the melted butter, almond extract and pinch of salt, then fold in the almonds and flour until well combined.

- Scrape the mixture into the prepared tin. Drizzle over the coulis and swirl over the surface with the tip of a knife.

- Bake in a preheated oven, 200°C (400°F), Gas Mark 6, for 18–20 minutes until golden and just firm to the touch.

- Leave to cool in the tin for 1–2 minutes, then lift on to a board using the lining paper and cut into 12–16 squares. Serve warm or cold with blackcurrant sorbet and scattered with toasted flaked almonds, if liked.

 Black Forest Blondie Pots

Place 300 g (10 oz) frozen forest fruits, 50 g (2 oz) soft light brown sugar and 1 teaspoon almond extract in a saucepan and heat gently until the fruit has collapsed. Leave to cool slightly. Meanwhile, put 150 g (5 oz) sliced shop-bought cherry Madeira loaf cake in 4 large ramekins and drizzle 1 tablespoon crème de mûres over each. Top each portion with 1 scoop of white chocolate ice cream. Spoon over the warm fruit and serve immediately, scattered with 25 g (1 oz) toasted flaked almonds.

 Blackcurrant Blondie Cupcakes

Place 2 large eggs and 125 g (4 oz) light soft brown sugar in a large bowl and whisk until combined, then beat in 125 g (4 oz) melted butter, 1 teaspoon vanilla extract, a pinch of salt, 75 g (3 oz) ground almonds, 50 g (2 oz) plain flour and 50 g (2 oz) white chocolate chips. Spoon the mixture into a 12-hole nonstick muffin tin lined with paper cupcake cases, then top each with 2 frozen blackcurrants. Bake in a preheated oven, 200°C (400°F), Gas Mark 6, for 12–14 minutes until golden. Serve warm or cold.

20 Cinnamon Crunch Cakes

Makes 12

50 g (2 oz) rolled oats
25 g (1 oz) demerara sugar
50 g (2 oz) chopped mixed nuts
25 g (1 oz) unsalted butter
23 cm (9 inch) shop-bought
    square, plain sponge cake or
    12 shop-bought plain cupcakes
1 teaspoon ground cinnamon
25 g (1 oz) dried blueberries

For the icing

75 g (3 oz) unsalted butter,
    softened
125 g (4 oz) icing sugar, sifted
1 teaspoon ground cinnamon
2 teaspoons coffee essence

- Mix together the oats, sugar and nuts in a large bowl. Heat the butter in a large, nonstick frying pan, add the oat mixture and toast over a medium-low heat for 6–8 minutes, stirring frequently until golden. Tip on to a plate and leave to cool.

- Meanwhile, make the icing. Place all the ingredients in a large bowl and beat together with a hand-held electric whisk until light and fluffy. Spread the buttercream over the sponge cake, then cut the cake into 12 squares. Alternatively, spread over 12 cupcakes.

- Stir the cinnamon and blueberries into the toasted oats, then sprinkle generously over the iced squares.

---

1 Cinnamon Butter Fancies

Make the buttercream icing as above. Cut a 300 g (10 oz) shop-bought all-butter Madeira loaf cake into 12 small squares, then use a small palette knife to spread the squares with the icing until the tops and sides are covered. Top each cake with a toasted blanched hazelnut.

3 Cinnamon Raisin Traybake

Place 125 g (4 oz) softened unsalted butter, 100 g (3½ oz) soft dark brown sugar, 125 g (4 oz) sifted self-raising flour, 1 teaspoon ground cinnamon, 1 teaspoon baking powder, 2 large lightly beaten eggs, 2 tablespoons runny honey, 1 tablespoon black treacle and 75 g (3 oz) raisins in a large bowl and beat together with a hand-held electric whisk until

pale and creamy. Spoon into a greased 30 x 20 cm (12 x 8 inch) brownie tin lined with nonstick baking paper and scatter over 50 g (2 oz) chopped mixed nuts. Bake in a preheated oven, 200°C (400°F), Gas Mark 6, for 20 minutes, or until risen and firm to the touch. Leave to cool in the tin for 1–2 minutes, then turn out on to a wire rack and peel away the lining paper. Serve warm or cold, cut into 12–16 squares.

CAK-CAKE-SAH

3 Oaty Flapjack Slice

Makes 12–16

200 g (7 oz) unsalted butter, plus extra for greasing
125 g (4 oz) demerara sugar
75 g (3 oz) agave nectar or honey
150 g (5 oz) sweetened condensed milk
325 g (11 oz) rolled oats
75 g (3 oz) self-raising flour
1 teaspoon mixed spice (optional)
pinch of salt

- Grease a 34 x 20 cm (12 x 8 inch) brownie tin and line with nonstick baking paper.

- Place the butter, sugar, agave nectar or honey and condensed milk in a large saucepan and heat gently, stirring occasionally, until the butter has melted and the sugar dissolved.

- Mix together the remaining ingredients in a large bowl, then pour into the warm syrup and stir until combined.

- Scrape the mixture into the prepared tin and bake in a preheated oven, 180°C (350°F), Gas Mark 4, for 15 minutes, or until pale golden.

- Leave to cool in the tin for 2–3 minutes, then mark into 12–16 squares or bars. Leave in the tin for a further 5 minutes until firm enough to handle, then transfer to a wire rack to cool completely.

 Flapjack Fingers with Chocolate Dip

Melt 100 g (3½ oz) plain dark chocolate, broken into small pieces, 125 ml (4 fl oz) double cream and 1 tablespoon golden syrup in a heatproof bowl set over a saucepan of gently simmering water, ensuring the bowl does not touch the water. Meanwhile, cut 4 shop-bought flapjacks into fingers. Serve with the chocolate sauce, for dipping.

 Oaty Flapjack Biscuits

Place 125 g (4 oz) unsalted butter, 2 tablespoons golden syrup and 175 g (6 oz) golden caster sugar in a saucepan and heat gently until melted. Meanwhile, mix together 150 g (5 oz) plain flour, 150 g (5 oz) rolled oats and 50 g (2 oz) raisins in a bowl. Place 1 teaspoon bicarbonate of soda in a small bowl and stir in 1 tablespoon boiling water. Add to the melted butter, then stir into the dry ingredients. Use lightly floured hands to roll the mixture into 20–25 walnut-sized balls, then place on 2 baking sheets lined with nonstick baking paper. Bake in a preheated oven, 200°C (400°F), Gas Mark 6, for 10–12 minutes until golden. Transfer to wire racks to cool.

30 Tropical Fruit and Coconut Blondies

Makes 12–16

150 g (5 oz) unsalted butter,
    melted, plus extra for greasing
2 large eggs
100 g (3½ oz) soft light
    brown sugar
75 g (3 oz) caster sugar
pinch of salt
125 g (4 oz) plain flour
75 g (3 oz) desiccated coconut
125 g (4 oz) ready-to-eat dried
    tropical fruit medley, chopped
mango sorbet, to serve (optional)

- Grease a 23 cm (9 inch) square brownie tin and line with nonstick baking paper (see page 9).

- Place the eggs, brown sugar and caster sugar in a large bowl and whisk until combined. Stir in the melted butter, salt, flour and coconut, then fold in the chopped tropical fruit.

- Scrape the mixture into the prepared tin and bake in a preheated oven, 200°C (400°F), Gas Mark 6, for 15–18 minutes until just firm to the touch.

- Leave to cool in the tin for 1–2 minutes, then lift on to a board using the lining paper and cut into 12–16 squares. Serve warm or cold, with mango sorbet, if liked.

---

 1 **Tropical Blondie Yogurt Pots**

Place 300 g (10 oz) frozen tropical fruits, 250 g (8 oz) Greek yogurt, 3 tablespoons coconut milk and 2 tablespoons honey in a food processor and blend until smooth. Cut 2 shop-bought blondies or thick slices of Madeira loaf cake into cubes and place in 4 deep ramekins or glasses. Pour 100 ml (3½ fl oz) ready-made mango coulis over the sponges and spoon over the yogurt mixture. Serve scattered with toasted coconut flakes or shavings.

 2 **Tropical Sorbet Blondies**

Place 300 g (10 oz) frozen tropical fruits, 75 ml (3 fl oz) freshly squeezed orange or pineapple juice, 1 tablespoon coconut rum and 2 tablespoons runny honey in a food processor and blend until very thick but smooth, then scrape into a shallow container and freeze for 10–15 minutes. Meanwhile, place 4 shop-bought blondies or chocolate brownies in 4 serving dishes. Place 2 tablespoons coconut shavings in a small, dry frying pan and gently toast for

2–3 minutes until pale golden. Top each blondie with 2 scoops of the sorbet and scatter over the toasted coconut. Serve drizzled with extra rum, if liked.

30 Banana and Walnut Fudge Brownies

Makes 12–16

175 g (6 oz) unsalted butter, plus extra for greasing

200 g (7 oz) plain dark chocolate, broken into small pieces

2 tablespoons dulce de leche or thick caramel sauce

3 large eggs

75 g (3 oz) soft light brown sugar

100 g (3½ oz) golden caster sugar

75 g (3 oz) self-raising flour

pinch of salt

50 g (2 oz) baking fudge chunks

50 g (2 oz) walnuts, chopped

50 g (2 oz) semi-dried banana, chopped

25 g (1 oz) sweetened dried banana chips, broken into pieces

- Grease a 30 x 20 cm (12 x 8 inch) brownie tin and line with nonstick baking paper (see page 9). Place the butter, chocolate and dulce de leche or caramel sauce in a small saucepan over a low heat and warm until just melted.

- Meanwhile, place the eggs, brown sugar and caster sugar in a large bowl and whisk until combined. Using a rubber spatula, stir in the melted chocolate mixture, flour, salt, fudge chunks, walnuts and semi-dried banana.

- Scrape the mixture into the prepared tin and scatter over the banana chips. Bake in a preheated oven, 200°C (400°F), Gas Mark 6, for 18–20 minutes until just firm to the touch.

- Leave to cool in the tin for 1–2 minutes, then lift on to a board using the lining paper and cut into 12–16 squares. Serve warm or cold.

---

10 Banoffee Brownies

Place 4 shop-bought chocolate brownies in 4 serving dishes and spread each thickly with 1 tablespoon dulce de leche or thick caramel sauce and top with ½ small banana, sliced. Whip 100 ml (3½ fl oz) double cream and 1 teaspoon vanilla bean paste in a bowl with a hand-held electric whisk until it forms soft peaks, then spoon over the sliced bananas. Scatter over 25 g (1 oz) sweetened dried banana chips and decorate with plain dark chocolate shavings.

20 Baked Brownie Banana Splits

Place 25 g (1 oz) unsalted butter and 2 tablespoons honey in a small saucepan over a low heat and warm until just melted, then stir in 1 teaspoon vanilla bean paste. Cut a slit down 4 large unpeeled bananas and fill with 2 sliced shop-bought chocolate brownies, then place on 4 large squares of foil. Drizzle over the warm honey mixture and wrap up in the foil. Bake in a preheated oven, 220°C (425°F), Gas Mark 7, for 10 minutes, or until the banana skins are blackened. Remove from the foil and place in 4 serving dishes. Crumble over 1 shop-bought chocolate brownie and serve with whipped cream.

Devonshire Cream Scones

Makes 6

6 shop-bought all-butter scones

6 tablespoons Devonshire clotted cream

6 tablespoons good-quality strawberry or raspberry jam

- Put the scones on a baking sheet and place in a preheated oven, 220°C (425°F), Gas Mark 7, for 2–3 minutes until warmed through.

- Split the scones open and top the bottom halve with a dollop of cream. Drizzle with the jam, replace the tops and serve.

---

 2 Homemade Scones and Cream

Sift 325 g (11 oz) self-raising flour and 2 teaspoons baking powder into a bowl. Add 75 g (3 oz) softened unsalted butter and rub in with the fingertips until the mixture resembles fine breadcrumbs. Stir in 2 tablespoons golden caster sugar. Whisk together 1 large egg, 1 large egg yolk and 125 ml (4 fl oz) milk in a jug. Pour into the dry ingredients, reserving about 1 tablespoon for glazing, and mix to form a soft but not sticky dough. Roll out on a floured surface to 1.5 cm (¾ inch) thick, then stamp out about 10 rounds using a 6 cm (2½ inch) plain cutter, without twisting the cutter. Place on 2 baking sheets lined with nonstick baking paper, brush lightly with the reserved glaze and bake in a preheated oven, 220°C (425°F), Gas Mark 7, for 12 minutes, or until risen and golden. Transfer to a wire rack to cool slightly, then serve as above.

3 Drop Scones with Clotted Cream

Sift 250 g (8 oz) self-raising flour, 1½ teaspoons baking powder and ½ teaspoon ground cinnamon or mixed spice into a bowl, then stir in 50 g (2 oz) golden caster sugar and make a well in the centre. Whisk together 2 large eggs and 200 ml (7 fl oz) milk in a jug, then pour into the well. Whisk together, gradually incorporating the flour from the edges until the batter is smooth. Heat 15 g (½ oz) butter in a large, nonstick frying pan, add small ladlefuls of the batter and cook for 2–3 minutes until bubbles start to appear on the surface, then flip over and cook until golden. Repeat with the remaining batter to make 18–20 drop scones, adding more butter to the pan if necessary. Serve warm with clotted cream and strawberry jam.

 # Toffee Apple Mini Traybakes

Makes 12

125 g (4 oz) unsalted butter, softened, plus extra for greasing

125 g (4 oz) self-raising flour

1 teaspoon baking powder

1 teaspoon ground cinnamon

¼ teaspoon ground nutmeg

½ teaspoon ground ginger

75 g (3 oz) soft dark brown sugar

50 g (2 oz) caster sugar

2 large eggs, lightly beaten

crème fraîche, to serve (optional)

For the toffee apples

50 g (2 oz) demerara sugar

50 g (2 oz) unsalted butter

2 teaspoons lemon juice

3 dessert apples, peeled, cored and sliced

- Grease a 12-hole individual traybake tray or nonstick muffin tin. Sift the flour, baking powder and spices into a large bowl. Add the remaining ingredients and beat together with a hand-held electric whisk until smooth and creamy.

- Spoon the mixture into the prepared tin and bake in a preheated oven, 200°C (400°F), Gas Mark 6, for 12–15 minutes until risen and firm to the touch.

- Meanwhile, make the toffee apples. Place the sugar, butter and lemon juice in a nonstick frying pan over a medium heat and heat until melted. Add the apples and simmer gently for 7–8 minutes, turning occasionally, until golden and softened. Leave to cool slightly.

- Remove the cakes from the oven and transfer to wire racks to cool slightly. Serve warm, topped with the toffee apples and sauce, and with crème fraîche, if liked.

 ### Toffee Apple Sponge Desserts

Mix together 2 grated dessert apples, 2 teaspoons lemon juice, 2 tablespoons soft dark brown sugar and 1 teaspoon ground cinnamon. Divide 6 broken up trifle sponge fingers between 4 tall serving glasses, spoon the grated apple over the biscuits, then drizzle 2 tablespoons ready-made toffee sauce over each. Whip 100 ml (3½ fl oz) double cream, 1 tablespoon sifted icing sugar and ½ teaspoon ground cinnamon, then spoon over the desserts. Serve immediately.

 ### Apple Pie Traybake

Place 125 g (4 oz) softened unsalted butter, 125 g (4 oz) golden caster sugar, 2 large lightly beaten eggs, ¼ teaspoon salt and 2 teaspoons finely grated lemon rind in a large bowl, then sift in 125 g (4 oz) self-raising flour, 1 teaspoon baking powder, 1 teaspoon cinnamon and 1 teaspoon mixed spice. Beat together with a hand-held electric whisk until pale and creamy. Fold in 1 peeled, cored and grated dessert apple. Scrape the mixture into a greased 23 cm (9 inch) square brownie tin lined with nonstick baking paper. Mix ½ teaspoon ground cinnamon and 2 tablespoons demerara sugar in a small bowl, then sprinkle over the mixture. Bake in a preheated oven, 200°C (400°F), Gas Mark 6, for 20–22 minutes until risen and golden. Turn out of the tin on to a wire rack and peel away the lining paper. Leave to cool slightly, then cut into 12–16 squares and serve with whipped cream or ice cream, if liked.

Pecan Cream Brownie Bites

Makes 16

75 g (3 oz) unsalted butter, softened

125 g (4 oz) icing sugar, sifted

1 teaspoon milk

1 teaspoon coffee essence

25 g (1 oz) pecan nuts, chopped, plus 16 pecan halves to decorate

4 shop-bought chocolate brownies, cut into quarters

- Place the butter, icing sugar and milk in a large bowl and beat together with a hand-held electric whisk until light and fluffy. Add the coffee essence and beat until evenly combined. Fold in the chopped pecans.

- Carefully spread the buttercream on to the brownie squares and top each with a pecan half.

 Pecan Brownie 'Pick-Me-Ups'

Stir 1 tablespoon demerara sugar into 75 ml (3 fl oz) strong, hot espresso coffee until dissolved, then add 1 tablespoon coffee liqueur. Cut up 4 chocolate brownies and arrange in 4 bowls, then drizzle over the coffee. Beat together 175 g (6 oz) mascarpone cheese, 125 ml (4 fl oz) double cream, 1 teaspoon each of vanilla extract and coffee extract and 75 g (3 oz) caster sugar in a bowl until thick. Fold in 25 g (1 oz) chopped pecan nuts. Spoon over the brownies, cover and chill for 5–10 minutes. Meanwhile, blitz 50 g (2 oz) pecan nuts and 25 g (1 oz) demerara sugar in a mini food processor until finely chopped. Serve the pecan sugar sprinkled over the brownies.

 Pecan Fudge Brownies

Place 150 g (5 oz) unsalted butter and 200 g (7 oz) plain dark chocolate, broken into small pieces, in a saucepan over a low heat and warm until just melted. Meanwhile, whisk 2 large eggs, 75 g (3 oz) golden caster sugar, 75 g (3 oz) soft light brown sugar and 2 teaspoons coffee essence in a bowl until combined. Using a rubber spatula, stir in 50 g (2 oz) self-raising flour, 75 g (3 oz) chopped pecan nuts and the melted chocolate. Scrape the mixture into a greased 30 x 20 cm (12 x 8 inch) brownie tin lined with nonstick baking paper (see page 9) and bake in a preheated oven, 200°C (400°F), Gas Mark 6, for 15–18 minutes until just firm to the touch, but with a slightly fudgy texture. Leave to cool in the tin for 1–2 minutes, then lift on to a board using the lining paper and cut into 12–16 squares. Serve warm or cold.

Blueberry, Cinnamon and Honey Welsh Cakes

Makes 14–16

225 g (7½ oz) self-raising flour, plus extra for dusting
1 teaspoon ground cinnamon
100 g (3½ oz) unsalted butter, softened, plus extra for frying
pinch of salt
50 g (2 oz) caster sugar
75 g (3 oz) dried blueberries
1 large egg, lightly beaten
2 tablespoons runny honey, plus extra to serve

- Sift the flour and cinnamon into a large bowl. Add the butter and rub in with the fingertips until the mixture resembles fine breadcrumbs, then stir in the salt, sugar and blueberries. Add the egg and honey and mix to form a soft but not sticky dough.

- Turn the dough out on to a floured surface and roll out to 5 mm (¼ inch) thick, then stamp out 14–16 rounds using a 7 cm (3 inch) plain cutter.

- Heat a knob of butter in a large, heavy-based frying pan, add the rounds and cook over a low heat for 2–3 minutes, then flip over and cook for a further 2–3 minutes until risen and golden. Repeat with the remaining rounds, adding a little more butter to the pan if necessary.

- Serve warm, drizzled with extra honey.

Cinnamon and Honey Iced Fingers

Sift 50 g (2 oz) icing sugar and ½ teaspoon ground cinnamon into a bowl. Add 1 tablespoon runny honey and mix to a smooth consistency, adding 1 teaspoon milk if necessary. Spread evenly over 6–8 finger buns and leave in a cool place for a few minutes to set. Meanwhile, mix together 1 tablespoon caster sugar and ½–1 teaspoon ground cinnamon, according to taste. Serve the buns dusted with a little cinnamon sugar.

Cinnamon and Honey Iced Scones

Sift 225 g (7½ oz) self-raising flour, 2 teaspoons baking powder and 1 teaspoon ground cinnamon into a large bowl. Add 50 g (2 oz) softened unsalted butter and rub in with the fingertips until the mixture resembles fine breadcrumbs, then stir in 2 tablespoons golden caster sugar, a pinch of salt and 75 g (3 oz) blueberries. Make a well in the centre and pour in 125 ml (4 fl oz) buttermilk, then mix to form a soft but not sticky dough. Roll out on a floured surface to 1.5 cm (¾ inch) thick, then stamp out about 8 rounds using a 7 cm (3 inch) fluted cutter. Place on a large baking sheet lined with nonstick baking paper and bake in a preheated oven, 220°C (425°F), Gas Mark 7, for 10 minutes, or until risen and golden. Meanwhile, place 50 g (2 oz) sifted icing sugar, 1½ tablespoons runny honey and 1–2 teaspoons apple juice in a bowl and mix to form a smooth paste. Transfer the scones to a wire rack and drizzle over the icing. Serve warm.

CAK-CAKE-LEU

Meringue Blondies with Boozy Cherries

Serves 6

2 large egg whites

100 g (3½ oz) caster sugar

6 shop-bought blondies or thick slices of Madeira loaf cake

150 g (5 oz) canned pitted black cherries in syrup, drained

For the boozy cherries

150 g (5 oz) canned pitted black cherries in syrup, drained

1 teaspoon finely grated lemon rind

2 teaspoons lemon juice

3 tablespoons kirsch or cherry brandy

75 g (3 oz) caster sugar

- Line a large baking sheet with nonstick baking paper. Whisk the egg whites and sugar in a clean bowl until the mixture forms soft peaks.

- Place the blondies or Madeira slices on the prepared baking sheet and pile the cherries on to the cakes. Spoon the meringue mixture over the cherries in attractive peaks.

- Bake in a preheated oven, 180°C (350°F), Gas Mark 4, for 10–12 minutes until pale golden.

- Meanwhile, make the boozy cherries. Place all the ingredients in a saucepan and heat gently, stirring occasionally, until the sugar has dissolved. Increase the heat and simmer gently for 5–6 minutes until slightly syrupy. Spoon into 6 serving dishes.

- Remove the blondies from the oven and lift on to the cherries using a wide spatula. Serve immediately.

 Cherry Brownies with Boozy Sauce

Place 150 g (5 oz) good-quality white chocolate, broken into small pieces, 150 ml (¼ pint) double cream, 2 tablespoons kirsch and the seeds scraped from 1 vanilla pod in a small saucepan over a low heat and warm until the chocolate has just melted, then stir gently. Place 6 warmed shop-bought brownies in 6 serving dishes and pour over the melted chocolate. Serve scattered with 150 g (5 oz) pitted cherries.

 Boozy Cherry Almond Blondies

Place 2 large eggs, 175 g (6 oz) caster sugar, 2 tablespoons kirsch or cherry brandy, 125 g (4 oz) melted unsalted butter, 1 teaspoon almond extract and a pinch of salt in a large bowl and whisk until combined. Fold in 150 g (5 oz) plain flour, then scrape the mixture into a greased 23 cm (9 inch) square brownie tin lined with nonstick baking paper (see page 9). Scatter over 75 g (3 oz) canned pitted black cherries in syrup, drained and halved, and 25 g (1 oz) flaked almonds. Bake in a preheated oven, 200°C (400°F), Gas Mark 6, for 18–22 minutes until golden. Meanwhile, make the Boozy Cherries as above. Leave the blondies to cool in the tin for 1–2 minutes, then lift on to a board using the lining paper and cut into 12–16 squares. Serve warm or cold with the cherries.

30 Peanut Butter Swirl Brownies

Makes 12–16

175 g (6 oz) unsalted butter, plus extra for greasing

200 g (7 oz) plain dark chocolate, broken into small pieces

75 g (3 oz) crunchy peanut butter

125 g (4 oz) smooth peanut butter

3 large eggs

175 g (6 oz) caster sugar

¼ teaspoon salt

50 g (2 oz) self-raising flour

- Grease a 30 x 20 cm (12 x 8 inch) brownie tin and line with nonstick baking paper (see page 9). Place the butter, chocolate and crunchy peanut butter in a small saucepan over a low heat and warm until just melted. In a separate saucepan, gently warm through the smooth peanut butter.

- Meanwhile, place the eggs, sugar and salt in a large bowl and whisk until combined. Using a rubber spatula, stir in the melted chocolate mixture and flour.

- Scrape the mixture into the prepared tin. Drizzle over the smooth peanut butter in 3–4 straight lines, then 'drag' through the peanut butter with the tip of a sharp knife to create a marbled effect.

- Bake in a preheated oven, 200°C (400°F), Gas Mark 6, for 18–20 minutes until just firm to the touch, but with a slightly fudgy texture. Leave to cool in the tin for 1–2 minutes, then lift on to a board using the lining paper and cut into 12–16 squares. Serve warm or cold.

 Peanut and Fudge Brownie Ice Creams

Place 50 g (2 oz) blanched, unsalted peanuts in a dry frying pan and toast over a medium-low heat, shaking frequently until golden. Tip on to a plate and leave to cool. Meanwhile, place 100 g (3½ oz) all-butter fudge and 150 ml (¼ pint) double cream in a small saucepan over a low heat and warm gently, stirring frequently, until smooth. Put the peanuts in a freezer bag and tap lightly with a rolling pin until roughly crushed. Remove the cream from the heat and stir in the peanuts. Chop 2 chilled shop-bought chocolate brownies into 1 cm (½ inch) cubes, then place in a bowl with 500 ml (17 fl oz) soft scoop vanilla or chocolate ice cream and mash together. Scoop into 4–6 serving dishes, then drizzle over the peanut fudge sauce and serve immediately.

 Peanut Butter Brownie Cupcakes

Melt 100 g (3½ oz) unsalted butter, 150 g (5 oz) plain dark chocolate and 75 g (2 oz) crunchy peanut butter in a saucepan. Meanwhile, whisk 2 large eggs and 125 g (4 oz) golden caster sugar until combined. Stir in the melted chocolate mixture and 75 g (3 oz) self-raising flour. Spoon into a 12-hole muffin tin lined with paper cases and scatter over 50 g (2 oz) chocolate chips. Bake in a preheated oven, 200°C (400°F), Gas Mark 6, for 10–12 minutes until almost firm to the touch.

Maple Frosted Walnut Slice

Makes 1 loaf cake

1 shop-bought loaf cake, such as walnut or Madeira, about 300 g (10 oz)

walnut halves, to decorate

For the frosting

75 g (3 oz) cream cheese

25 g (1 oz) unsalted butter, softened

2 tablespoons maple syrup

1 teaspoon vanilla extract

75 g (3 oz) icing sugar

- To make the frosting, place the cream cheese, butter, maple syrup and vanilla extract in a large bowl and beat with a hand-held electric whisk until very pale and creamy. Gradually sift in the icing sugar, beating well between each addition.

- Use a small palette knife to spread the frosting thickly over the loaf cake, then decorate with walnut halves. Serve the cake cut into thick slices.

 Coffee and Walnut Trifles

Stir 2 tablespoons maple syrup into 75 ml (3 fl oz) hot, strong, Italian-style coffee. Arrange 8 broken sponge fingers in the bottom of 4 glass serving dishes, then pour over the hot coffee, reserving 2 tablespoons, and set aside. Whip 100 ml (3½ fl oz) double cream, 200 g (7 oz) mascarpone cheese, the reserved coffee and 2 tablespoons caster sugar in a bowl with a hand-held electric whisk until thick and creamy, then spoon over the sponge fingers. Cover and chill for 10 minutes. Serve scattered with 25 g (1 oz) chopped walnuts and dusted generously with sweetened cocoa powder.

 Walnut Sandwich Sponge

Place 125 g (4 oz) each of softened unsalted butter, golden caster sugar and sifted self-raising flour, 1 teaspoon baking powder, 2 large lightly beaten eggs, 2 teaspoons coffee essence and 1–2 tablespoons milk in a large bowl and beat together with a hand-held electric whisk until pale and creamy. Divide the mixture between 2 greased 20 cm (8 inch) round cake tins lined with nonstick baking paper and bake in a preheated oven, 200°C (400°F), Gas Mark 6, for 15–18 minutes until risen and firm to the touch. Turn the cakes out of the tins on to a wire rack, peel away the lining paper and leave to cool. Meanwhile, make double the quantity of frosting as above. Spread half the frosting over one of the cakes and sandwich the two together, then spread the top with the remaining frosting. Decorate with walnut halves and chocolate curls.

CAK-CAKE-VIA

Quick Coconut Lamingtons

Makes 12

20 cm (8 inch) square sponge cake or 300 g (10 oz) Madeira loaf cake, 1-day-old
175 g (6 oz) shredded coconut
375 g (12 oz) icing sugar, sifted
50 ml (2 fl oz) boiling water
50 ml (2 fl oz) warm milk, plus extra if needed
few drops of red food colouring (optional)

- Cut the cake into 12 squares. Scatter the coconut over a plate.

- Place the icing sugar in a heatproof bowl and beat in the boiling water and milk until the mixture is smooth and runny, adding a little more milk, if necessary. Add the food colouring, if using, to make a pink icing. Place the bowl over a saucepan of hot but not boiling water to keep the icing runny.

- Use 2 forks to dip 1 sponge square into the pink icing, making sure that it is completely coated, then roll it gently in the coconut until covered. Transfer to a wire rack to set. Repeat with the remaining sponge squares.

 Iced Coconut Cream Squares

Place 200 g (7 oz) white chocolate in a food processor and blitz until finely chopped, then transfer to a heatproof bowl. Heat 75 ml (3 fl oz) double cream in a saucepan until almost boiling, then pour over the chocolate and stir until melted. Stir in 50 g (2 oz) desiccated coconut, then chill for 4–5 minutes. Spread the chocolate cream over a 20 cm (8 inch) shop-bought square sponge cake, then cut into 12 squares. Serve sprinkled with extra desiccated coconut.

 Cherry Coconut Cake

Place 125 g (4 oz) softened unsalted butter, 75 g (3 oz) soft light brown sugar, 50 g (2 oz) golden caster sugar, 125 g (4 oz) sifted self-raising flour, 1 teaspoon baking powder, 50 g (2 oz) desiccated coconut, 2 large lightly beaten eggs, 1 teaspoon coconut or almond extract and 1 teaspoon finely grated lemon rind in a large bowl and beat together with a hand-held electric whisk until pale and creamy. Spoon the mixture into a greased 23 cm (9 inch) square cake tin lined with nonstick baking paper and scatter over 50 g (2 oz) halved glacé cherries. Bake in a preheated oven, 200°C (400°F), Gas Mark 6, for 20–22 minutes until risen and firm to the touch. Turn out of the tin on to a wire rack, peel away the lining paper and leave to cool.

Banana and Chocolate Pancakes

Makes about 20

125 g (4 oz) self-raising flour
75 g (3 oz) wholemeal plain flour
2 teaspoons baking powder
50 g (2 oz) soft light brown sugar
2 large eggs, lightly beaten
125 ml (4 fl oz) milk
2 tablespoons Irish cream liqueur
 or milk
2 small, ripe bananas, roughly
 mashed
50 g (2 oz) milk or plain dark
 chocolate chips
15 g (½ oz) butter
vegetable oil, for frying

To serve

vanilla ice cream
warmed chocolate sauce
 (optional)

- Sift the flours and baking powder into a large bowl, then stir in the sugar and make a well in the centre. Whisk together the eggs, milk and liqueur, if using, in a jug, then pour into the well. Whisk together, gradually incorporating the flour from the edges until the batter is smooth. Stir in the mashed bananas and chocolate chips.

- Heat the butter and a little oil in a large, nonstick frying pan, add small ladlefuls of the batter and cook for 2–3 minutes until bubbles start to appear on the surface, then flip over and cook for a further 30–60 seconds until golden. Repeat with the remaining batter to make about 20 small pancakes, adding more butter and oil to the pan if necessary.

- Serve warm with scoops of ice cream and drizzled with warmed chocolate sauce, if liked.

 Banana and Choc Muffin Splits

Whip 100 ml (3½ fl oz) whipping cream in a bowl with a hand-held electric whisk until it forms soft peaks. Cut 4 bananas in half lengthways and arrange in 4 serving dishes. Top each one with 1 scoop of ice cream and a dollop of the whipped cream. Crumble half a chocolate muffin over each one and serve immediately.

 Banana Chocolate Rockcakes

Sift 150 g (5 oz) self-raising flour, 100 g (3½ oz) wholemeal self-raising flour, 1½ teaspoons baking powder and 1 teaspoon ground cinnamon into a bowl. Add 125 g (4 oz) softened unsalted butter and rub in with the fingertips until the mixture resembles fine breadcrumbs. Place 50 g (2 oz) sweetened dried banana chips in a small freezer bag and tap with a rolling pin until broken into small pieces. Stir the banana chips, 100 g (3½ oz) granulated sugar and 75 g (3 oz) chocolate chips into the flour mixture. Add 1 mashed banana, 1 large beaten egg and enough of 1–2 tablespoons milk to mix a stiff, sticky mixture. Drop 10–12 rough-surfaced mounds of the mixture on to 2 baking sheets lined with nonstick baking paper and bake in a preheated oven, 200°C (400°F), Gas Mark 6, for 18–20 minutes until golden. Transfer to wire racks to cool slightly, then serve warm.

3 Orange and Hazelnut Crumble Cake

Makes 1 x 23 cm (9 inch) cake

150 g (5 oz) unsalted butter, softened, plus extra for greasing
125 g (4 oz) golden caster sugar
100 g (3½ oz) self-raising flour, sifted
1 teaspoon baking powder
50 g (2 oz) ground hazelnuts
2 large eggs, lightly beaten
2 teaspoons finely grated orange rind, plus extra to decorate
1 teaspoon orange extract
125 g (4 oz) ready-made crumble mix
mascarpone cheese, to serve

- Grease a 23 cm (9 inch) square cake tin and line with nonstick baking paper.

- Place all of the ingredients except the crumble mix in a large bowl and beat together with a hand-held electric whisk until pale and creamy. Spoon the mixture into the prepared tin and sprinkle over the crumble mix.

- Bake in a preheated oven, 200°C (400°F), Gas Mark 6, for 22 minutes, or until golden and firm to the touch. Turn out of the tin on to a wire rack and peel away the lining paper.

- Serve warm or cold with mascarpone, decorated with orange rind.

1 Orange and Hazelnut Crunch

Heat 25 g (1 oz) unsalted butter in a frying pan, add 50 g (2 oz) ground hazelnuts, 50 g (2 oz) crumbled shop-bought Madeira cake and 25 g (1 oz) demerara sugar and cook gently for 6–7 minutes until toasted and golden. Tip into a bowl and leave to cool slightly. Meanwhile, place 200 g (7 oz) mascarpone cheese, 2 tablespoons chocolate hazelnut spread, 2 teaspoons grated orange rind, 2 tablespoons orange liqueur and 125 ml (4 fl oz) double cream in a bowl and beat with a hand-held electric whisk until thick and creamy. Divide between 4 glasses and sprinkle over the topping. Serve immediately.

2 Orange and Hazelnut Sponge

Cheesecakes Crumble 125 g (4 oz) shop-bought plain sponge or Madeira loaf cake until it resembles breadcrumbs, then mix together with 50 g (2 oz) ground hazelnuts and 50 g (2 oz) melted unsalted butter in a bowl. Divide between 4 glass serving dishes. Beat together 200 g (7 oz) cream cheese, 2 teaspoons finely grated orange rind, 150 ml (¼ pint) Greek yogurt and 1–2 tablespoons runny honey in a bowl. Divide the mixture between the glasses, then cover and chill for 10 minutes, or until required. Serve scattered with 25 g (1 oz) chopped toasted hazelnuts.

30 Cookie Dough Brownies

Makes 12–16

150 g (5 oz) unsalted butter, plus extra for greasing

150 g (5 oz) plain dark chocolate, broken into small pieces

2 large eggs

125 g (4 oz) caster sugar

50 g (2 oz) self-raising flour

pinch of salt

200 g (7 oz) shop-bought chilled cookie dough, chopped

50 ml (2 fl oz) sweetened condensed milk

· Grease a 30 x 20 cm (12 x 8 inch) brownie tin and line with nonstick baking paper (see page 9). Place the butter and chocolate in a small saucepan over a low heat and warm until just melted.

· Meanwhile, place the eggs and sugar in a large bowl and whisk until combined. Using a rubber spatula, stir in the melted chocolate, flour, salt and cookie dough.

· Scrape the mixture into the prepared tin and drizzle over the condensed milk.

· Bake in a preheated oven, 200°C (400°F), Gas Mark 6, for 15–18 minutes until just firm to the touch, but with a slightly fudgy texture.

· Leave to cool in the tin for 1–2 minutes, then lift on to a board using the lining paper and cut into 12–16 squares. Serve warm or cold.

 Cookie Cream Frosted Brownies

Beat together 150 g (5 oz) cream cheese, 3 tablespoons double cream, 25 g (1 oz) vanilla sugar, 75 g (3 oz) crushed chocolate cream cookies, such as chocolate bourbons, and 25 g (1 oz) finely chopped or grated milk chocolate in a large bowl. Spoon the frosting into a piping bag fitted with a plain nozzle, then pipe on to 4–6 shop-bought chocolate brownies. Crumble 1 chocolate cream cookie over each brownie, then serve.

 Cookie Dough Choc Brownie

Pudding Arrange 4 halved shop-bought chocolate brownies in a medium-sized, ovenproof dish and scatter over 50 g (2 oz) chopped walnuts, 50 g (2 oz) baking fudge chunks and 100 g (3½ oz) shop-bought chilled cookie dough, chopped. Pour over 300 g (10 oz) shop-bought Belgian chocolate sauce. Bake in a preheated oven, 200°C (400°F), Gas Mark 6, for 10–12 minutes until bubbling. Serve with ice cream.

QuickCook
Savoury Bakes

Recipes listed by cooking time

3(clock)

2(clock)

30 Herb and Seed Scottish Oatcakes

Makes 14–16

125 g (4 oz) wholemeal plain flour, plus extra for dusting

½ teaspoon salt

pinch of bicarbonate of soda

150 g (5 oz) fine oat bran or fine oatmeal

1 teaspoon dried herbs, such as thyme, rosemary or chives

3 tablespoons mixed seeds, such as pumpkin, sunflower, sesame and linseeds

50 g (2 oz) lard or unsalted butter, melted

3–4 tablespoons cold water

To serve

tomato chutney

Cheddar cheese

· Line 2 baking sheets with nonstick baking paper. Sift the flour, salt and bicarbonate of soda into a bowl, then mix in the oat bran or fine oatmeal, herbs and seeds. Make a well in the centre and pour in the melted lard or butter. Mix until combined, adding enough of the measurement water to form a soft but not sticky dough.

· Turn the dough out on to a floured surface and roll out to 2–3 mm (⅛ inch) thick, then stamp out 14–16 rounds using an 8 cm (3½ inch) plain cutter.

· Place the rounds on the prepared baking sheets and bake in a preheated oven, 200°C (400°F), Gas Mark 6, for 18–20 minutes until crisp and lightly golden. Transfer to wire racks to cool. Serve with tomato chutney and Cheddar cheese.

---

1 Herb and Seed Sandwich Biscuits

Place 125 g (4 oz) cream cheese, 2 tablespoons chopped mixed herbs, such as thyme, chives, basil or parsley, and 3 tablespoons mixed seeds in a bowl. Season with a little salt and pepper, then beat until smooth. Spread the mixture over 8 oatcakes, then top each with a second biscuit and sandwich together.

2 Herb and Seed Crackers

Place 50 g (2 oz) fine oat bran, 125 g (4 oz) plain flour, a pinch of salt, 1 teaspoon dried herbs and 3 tablespoons mixed seeds or sesame seeds in a bowl and mix until combined. Make a well in the centre and add 3 tablespoons olive or infused oil and enough cold water to form a firm dough. Roll out on a floured surface to 2–3 mm (⅛ inch) thick, then stamp out 18–20 rounds using a 6 cm (2½ inch) plain cutter. Place on 2 baking sheets lined with nonstick baking paper and bake in a preheated oven, 200°C (400°F), Gas Mark 6, for 12–15 minutes until crisp and golden. Transfer to wire racks to cool.

30 Tear and Share Masala Scones

Makes 8–10

300 g (10 oz) self-raising flour
2 teaspoons garam masala
1 teaspoon baking powder
1 teaspoon salt
75 g (3 oz) unsalted butter,
softened
100 g (3½ oz) Wensleydale or
Cheshire cheese, crumbled
2 finely chopped spring onions
2 tablespoons finely chopped
coriander leaves
¼ teaspoon ground black pepper
50 g (2 oz) spicy mango chutney
1 tablespoon lemon juice
75 ml (3 fl oz) milk
3 tablespoon natural yogurt
cumin seeds, black onion seeds or
curry leaves, for sprinkling

For the glaze

1 teaspoon spicy mango chutney
2 teaspoons milk (optional)

- Line a baking sheet with nonstick baking paper. Sift the flour, garam masala, baking powder and salt into a large bowl. Add the butter and rub in with the fingertips until the mixture resembles fine breadcrumbs, then stir in the cheese, spring onions, coriander and pepper.

- Mix together the mango chutney, lemon juice, milk and yogurt in a bowl, then pour into the dry ingredients and mix to form a soft dough.

- Turn the dough out on a floured surface and roll out gently to 1.5 cm (¾ inch) thick, then cut into 8–10 rounds or squares. Place close together on the baking sheet, so that the scones stick together during cooking.

- Mix together the glaze ingredients in a small bowl and brush over the scones, then sprinkle with a pinch of cumin seeds, black onion seeds or curry leaves. Bake in a preheated oven, 220°C (425°F), Gas Mark 7, for 18 minutes, or until risen and golden. Transfer to a wire rack to cool slightly, then serve the scones warm.

10 Baked Masala Naans

Mix 75 g (3 oz) crumbled Cheshire cheese, 2 teaspoons garam masala, 2 chopped spring onions, 2 tablespoons chopped coriander leaves, and 3 tablespoons natural yogurt. Split open 4 mini naan breads, and spread 1 cut side with mango chutney. Fill with the cheese, then bake in a preheated oven, 220°C (425°F), Gas Mark 7, for 4–5 minutes.

20 Masala Scones

Pulse 300 g (10 oz) self-raising flour, 1 teaspoon salt, 2 teaspoons garam masala, 1 teaspoon black mustard seeds, 1 teaspoon baking powder and 75 g (3 oz) cold, diced butter in a food processor until the mixture resembles breadcrumbs. Add 100 g (3½ oz) crumbled Cheshire cheese, 2 chopped spring onions, 2 tablespoons chopped coriander leaves, 50 g (2 oz) spicy mango chutney, 1 tablespoon lemon juice, 75 ml (3 fl oz) milk and 3 tablespoons natural yogurt and pulse to form a soft dough. Roll out to 1 cm (½ inch) thick, then stamp out 14–16 rounds using a 5 cm (2 inch) plain cutter. Place on 2 prepared baking sheets, then brush with the glaze as above and sprinkle over some black mustard seeds. Bake in a preheated oven, 230°C (450°F), Gas Mark 8, for 8–10 minutes until golden.

CAK-SAVO-ZYY

20 Pizza Palmiers

Makes 30–40

3 tablespoons ready-made
pizza sauce

25 g (1 oz) anchovies in oil,
drained and finely chopped

375 g (12 oz) chilled ready-rolled
puff pastry

1 teaspoon dried oregano

3 tablespoons finely grated
Parmesan cheese

- Line 2 large baking sheets with nonstick baking paper. Place the pizza sauce in a bowl and stir in the anchovies.

- Unroll the pastry on a clean surface and spread thinly with the pizza sauce. Scatter with the oregano and sprinkle the cheese evenly over the top. Roll the long sides of the pastry into the centre, then cut into 30–40 x 1 cm (½ inch) slices and place on the prepared baking sheets.

- Bake in a preheated oven, 220 °C (425 °F), Gas Mark 7, for 10–12 minutes until puffed up, crisp and golden. Transfer to wire racks to cool slightly, then serve warm.

10 Ciabatta Pizzas

Cut 1 large ciabatta loaf in half horizontally and cook under a preheated grill, cut sides up, for 1–2 minutes until golden. Spread 2 tablespoons ready-made pizza sauce over each cut side and divide 125 g (4 oz) thinly sliced mushrooms, 125 g (4 oz) sliced mozzarella cheese, 25 g (1 oz) anchovies in oil, drained and finely chopped, and 1 teaspoon dried oregano between the halves. Drizzle with olive oil and place in a preheated oven, 230 °C (450 °F), Gas Mark 8, for 6–8 minutes until bubbling and golden. Cut each ciabatta in half and serve with a tomato and rocket salad.

30 Puff Pizzas

Roll out 500 g (1 lb) chilled puff pastry on a floured surface and cut out 2 x 33 cm (13 inch) rounds, rerolling the trimmings if necessary. Place on 2 large nonstick baking sheets lined with nonstick baking paper and spread 2 tablespoons ready-made pizza sauce evenly over each base. Scatter over 125 g (4 oz) thinly sliced mushrooms, then top with 125 g (4 oz) crumbled or sliced goats' cheese and scatter 8 pitted Kalamata olives over each. Sprinkle over 1 teaspoon dried oregano and drizzle with 2 teaspoons olive oil. Bake in a preheated oven, 220 °C (425 °F), Gas Mark 7, for 15–18 minutes until puffed up and golden. Cut each pizza in half and serve with a tomato and mozzarella salad.

30 Seeded Goats' Cheese and Chive Muffins

Makes 12

50 g (2 oz) rolled oats

2 tablespoons mixed seeds

1 teaspoon salt

½ teaspoon freshly ground
black pepper

100 g (3½ oz) wholemeal
plain flour

100 g (3½ oz) plain flour

2 teaspoons baking powder

1 teaspoon bicarbonate of soda

1 small courgette, about 125 g
(4 oz), coarsely grated

2 large eggs, lightly beaten

75 ml (3 fl oz) vegetable oil

200 g (7 oz) natural yogurt

50 ml (2 fl oz) milk

2 tablespoons chopped chives

150 g (5 oz) soft goats' cheese,
crumbled

6 cherry tomatoes, halved

- Line a 12-hole nonstick muffin tin with paper muffin cases or lightly grease. Mix together the oats, seeds, salt and pepper in a large bowl, then sift in the flours, baking powder and bicarbonate of soda.

- Place the courgette in a clean cloth or tea towel and squeeze to remove the excess moisture. Whisk together the eggs, oil, yogurt, milk, courgette, chives and 100 g (3½ oz) of the goats' cheese in a jug or large bowl. Pour into the dry ingredients and stir until just combined.

- Spoon the mixture into the prepared muffin tin, then top each muffin with a halved cherry tomato and scatter over the remaining goats' cheese.

- Bake in a preheated oven, 180°C (350°F), Gas Mark 4, for 18–22 minutes until risen and golden. Serve warm.

---

10 Warm Goats' Cheese Muffin Salad

Slice 4 shop-bought savoury herb muffins thickly and top each piece with 1 slice of firm goats' cheese. Heat 2 tablespoons olive oil in a flame-proof frying pan, add the muffins, cheese side up, and cook for 1–2 minutes until the bases are golden. Cook under a preheated hot grill for 1–2 minutes until melting. Divide 200 g (7 oz) mixed salad leaves between 4 serving plates. Add the 'toasts' and drizzle with olive oil and balsamic vinegar.

20 Goats' Cheese and Chive Cupcakes

Sift 200 g (7 oz) self-raising flour, 1 teaspoon baking powder and ¼ teaspoon of salt into a large bowl, then stir in ½ teaspoon freshly ground black pepper, ½ teaspoon fennel seeds and 2 tablespoons chopped chives. Whisk together 1 large lightly beaten egg, 100 g (3½ oz) soft goats' cheese, crumbled, 75 g (3 oz) melted unsalted butter and 75 ml (3 fl oz) milk in a jug. Pour into the dry ingredients and stir until combined. Spoon the mixture into a 12-hole nonstick muffin tin lined with paper cupcake cases and bake in a preheated oven, 200°C (400°F), Gas Mark 6, for 12–15 minutes until risen, golden and firm to the touch. Serve the cupcakes warm.

30 Courgette and Feta Rockcakes

Makes 12–14

250 g (8 oz) self-raising flour

1½ teaspoons baking powder

1 teaspoon salt

125 g (4 oz) unsalted butter, softened

½ teaspoon finely grated lemon rind

½ teaspoon dried thyme

½ teaspoon ground black pepper

150 g (5 oz) courgette, coarsely grated

100 g (3½ oz) feta cheese, crumbled

1 large egg

1 tablespoon sun-dried tomato paste

4–5 tablespoons milk

- Line 2 baking sheets with nonstick baking paper. Sift the flour, baking powder and salt into a large bowl. Add the butter and rub in with the fingertips until the mixture resembles fine breadcrumbs, then stir in the lemon rind, thyme, pepper, courgette and feta.

- Whisk together the egg and tomato paste in a small bowl, then pour into the dry ingredients, adding just enough of the milk to form a soft, sticky mixture.

- Drop 12–14 rough-surfaced mounds of the mixture on to the prepared baking sheets.

- Bake in a preheated oven, 200°C (400°F), Gas Mark 6, for 18–20 minutes until golden. Serve warm.

Courgette and Feta Muffins

Cut 1 large courgette into long, thin slices and cook on a preheated hot griddle pan for 5–6 minutes, turning once, until softened and charred. Meanwhile, split 4 wholemeal English muffins in half and toast under a preheated grill. Spread 1 teaspoon sun-dried tomato paste over each cut side and layer over the courgette. Crumble over 100 g (3½ oz) feta cheese and return to the grill for 1 minute. Sprinkle with chopped thyme leaves and a squeeze of lemon juice. Serve warm with rocket leaves.

Courgette and Feta Mini Muffins

Sift 125 g (4 oz) plain flour, 1 teaspoon baking powder and ¼ teaspoon salt into a bowl. Add 50 g (2 oz) softened unsalted butter and rub in with the fingertips until the mixture resembles fine breadcrumbs. Finely grate 50 g (2 oz) courgette, then squeeze out the excess moisture and stir into the bowl with ¼ teaspoon dried thyme, 50 g (2 oz) crumbled feta cheese, ½ teaspoon ground black pepper and ½ teaspoon finely grated lemon rind. Whisk together 1 large egg, 75 ml (3 fl oz) milk, 75 ml (3 fl oz) vegetable oil and 1 tablespoon sun-dried tomato paste in a jug. Pour into the dry ingredients and stir until just combined. Spoon the mixture into about 18 holes of 2 well-greased 12-hole nonstick mini muffin tins and bake in a preheated oven, 200°C (400°F), Gas Mark 6, for 10–12 minutes until risen and golden.

Cream Cheese and Herb Toast Soufflés

Serves 4

4 large slices of rustic-style bread, such as sourdough

3 large eggs, separated

75 g (3 oz) cream cheese with garlic or herbs

3 tablespoons mixed chopped herbs, such as oregano, parsley, chives and dill

50 g (2 oz) Parmesan cheese, finely grated

salt and pepper

baby leaf and herb salad, to serve

- Toast the bread under a preheated hot grill for 1 minute on each side, or until toasted and golden.

- Meanwhile, beat together the egg yolks, cream cheese, herbs and cheese in a large bowl, then season with salt and pepper.

- Whisk the egg whites in a clean bowl with a hand-held electric whisk until they form soft peaks, then gently fold into the herby cream cheese mixture until just combined.

- Spoon the mixture over the hot toasts and cook under a preheated medium grill for 3–5 minutes until puffed up and golden.

- Serve with a baby leaf and herb salad.

---

2 Herby Souffléd Omelette

Beat together 3 large egg yolks, 125 g (4 oz) garlic and herb soft cheese, 1 tablespoon chopped herbs and 25 g (1 oz) grated Parmesan cheese, then season well. Whisk 3 egg whites until they form soft peaks, then fold into the cheese mixture. Heat 25 g (1 oz) butter in an ovenproof frying pan and cook the egg mixture gently for 2 minutes. Sprinkle over 1 tablespoon finely grated Parmesan, then bake in a preheated oven, 200°C (400°F), Gas Mark 6, for 10 minutes. Cut into 4 wedges, scatter with extra herbs and serve with salad.

3 Cream Cheese and Herb Soufflés

Place 25 g (1 oz) butter and 25 g (1 oz) plain flour in a saucepan over a medium heat and stir to form a paste, then cook for 1 minute and remove from the heat. Stir in 150 ml (¼ pint) milk, a little at a time. Return the pan to a low heat and bring slowly to the boil, stirring continuously until thickened. Pour into a large bowl and stir in 100 g (3½ oz) cream cheese, 2 tablespoons chopped herbs and 25 g (1 oz) grated Parmesan cheese, then 2 large egg yolks. Season with salt and pepper. Whisk 2 large egg whites in a clean bowl using a hand-held electric whisk until they form soft peaks, then fold into the cheese sauce. Gently spoon the mixture into 4 greased 200 ml (7 fl oz) ovenproof ramekins and bake in a preheated oven, 200°C (400°F), Gas Mark 6, for 15–18 minutes until risen and golden. Serve immediately.

Red Pepper and Goats' Cheese Quiches

Serves 4

325 g (11 oz) chilled ready-rolled shortcrust pastry

butter, for greasing

125 g (4 oz) roasted red peppers in oil, drained and sliced

125 g (4 oz) artichoke hearts in water or oil, drained and quartered

100 g (3½ oz) goats' cheese log, crumbled or diced

2 large eggs, lightly beaten

50 ml (2 fl oz) single cream

2 teaspoons chopped oregano leaves

salt and pepper

mixed salad leaves, to serve

- Unroll the pastry and cut out 4 x 12 cm (5 inch) rounds, then use to line 4 greased individual quiche tins or Yorkshire pudding tins, trimming away any excess pastry. Place the tins on a baking sheet.

- Divide the red peppers, artichokes and goats' cheese between the pastry cases. Whisk together the eggs, cream and oregano in a jug, then season and divide evenly between the cases.

- Bake in a preheated oven, 220°C (425°F), Gas Mark 7, for 15 minutes, or until the quiches are set and the pastry is golden.

- Serve warm or cold with mixed green salad.

 Breadsticks with Cheesy Pepper Dip

Cut 400 g (13 oz) chilled ready-rolled pizza dough into about 30 x 1 cm (½ inch) strips. Place on a prepared baking sheet, then drizzle with olive oil and sprinkle with 1 teaspoon each dried oregano and sea salt flakes. Bake in a preheated oven, 230°C (450°F), Gas Mark 8, for 4–5 minutes until crisp. Meanwhile, blend 100 g (3½ oz) goats' cheese, 75 g (3 oz) drained artichoke hearts in oil, 125 g (4 oz) roasted peppers in oil, drained and sliced, and 50 g (2 oz) cream cheese in a food processor until almost smooth. Serve with the breadsticks.

 Red Pepper and Goats' Cheese

Bricks Heat 2 tablespoons olive oil in a large, nonstick frying pan, add 2 cored, deseeded and thinly sliced red peppers and fry for 7–8 minutes until softened and lightly golden. Remove from the heat and sprinkle with 2 teaspoons chopped oregano leaves or 1 teaspoon dried oregano. Meanwhile, lay 4 sheets of feuilles de brick pastry on a clean surface. Divide 150 g (5 oz) artichoke hearts in water or oil, drained and sliced, between the sheets, then crumble over 100 g (3½ oz) goats' cheese and spoon the softened peppers on top.

Season well with black pepper, then fold the edges of the pastry into the centre, encasing the filling and creating 4 brick shapes. Place on a large baking sheet lined with nonstick baking paper and brush with a little olive oil or melted unsalted butter. Bake in a preheated oven, 200°C (400°F), Gas Mark 6, for 15 minutes, or until crisp and golden. Serve with a mixed green salad.

Black Pepper Savouries

Makes 20–22

125 g (4 oz) self-raising flour, plus extra for dusting
½ teaspoon dry mustard powder
pinch of salt
1 teaspoon cracked black pepper
50 g (2 oz) unsalted butter, softened
25 g (1 oz) mature Cheddar cheese, finely grated
1 large egg yolk
1 tablespoon water

- Line 2 baking sheets with nonstick baking paper. Mix together the flour, mustard powder, salt and black pepper in a bowl. Add the butter and rub in with the fingertips until the mixture resembles fine breadcrumbs. Stir in the cheese, then add the egg yolk and measurement water and mix to form a firm dough.

- Turn the dough out on to a floured surface and knead lightly. Roll out to 2–3 mm (⅛ inch) thick, then stamp out 20–22 rounds or shapes using a 5 cm (2 inch) cutter.

- Place the rounds on the prepared baking sheets and bake in a preheated oven, 200°C (400°F), Gas Mark 6, for 10 minutes, or until lightly golden. Transfer to wire racks to cool.

 Black Pepper and Parmesan Crackers

Place 12 Scottish oatcakes on a baking sheet and top each one with 1 teaspoon finely grated Parmesan cheese, a sprinkling of cracked black pepper and a pinch of ground cumin. Cook under a preheated grill for 2–3 minutes until bubbling and golden. Transfer to wire racks to cool slightly, then serve warm with seedless grapes.

Black Pepper and Cumin Biscuits

Toast 1 teaspoon cumin seeds in a small, dry pan for 2–3 minutes until aromatic, then transfer to a spice grinder or pestle and mortar and grind to a powder. Beat together 100 g (3½ oz) softened unsalted butter, ½ teaspoon dry mustard powder, the ground cumin seeds, a pinch of salt, 1 teaspoon cracked black pepper and 2 large egg yolks in a bowl. Add 25 g (1 oz) finely grated mature Cheddar cheese and 150 g (5 oz) self-raising flour and mix to form a soft but not sticky dough. Roll out on a floured surface to 2–3 mm (⅛ inch) thick, then cut into about 30 x 5 cm (2 inch) squares. Place on 2 large baking sheets lined with nonstick baking paper and brush with a little water or milk. Sprinkle a pinch of cumin seeds over each. Bake in a preheated oven, 200°C (400°F), Gas Mark 6, for 12 minutes, or until crisp and lightly golden. Transfer to wire racks to cool.

CAK-SAVO-SUE

30 Mini Sausage, Sage and Onion Rolls

Makes 12

375 g (12 oz) chilled ready-rolled puff pastry

2 tablespoons wholegrain or mild Dijon mustard

4 teaspoons chopped sage

4 spring onions, finely chopped

12 thin sausages, such as pork and leek chipolatas

beaten egg, to glaze

1–2 tablespoons finely grated Parmesan cheese (optional)

- Line 2 baking sheets with nonstick baking paper. Unroll the pastry on a clean surface and use a palette knife to spread the mustard thinly over the surface. Scatter over the chopped sage and spring onions.

- Use a pizza cutter or sharp knife to cut the pastry in half lengthways and then cut each half into 3 x 13 cm (5½ inch) squares. Place a sausage on the edge of 1 pastry square, then roll up until the sausage is just covered. Add a second sausage and continue to roll until you are left with a cylindrical, double-sausage roll. Cut the roll in half to create 2 mini rolls, then score 2 diagonal lines on top of each one. Repeat with the remaining pastry and sausages.

- Place the sausage rolls on the prepared baking sheets and brush with beaten egg. Sprinkle with a little cheese, if using, and bake in a preheated oven, 220°C (425°F), Gas Mark 7, for 15–18 minutes until the sausages are cooked through and the pastry is puffed up and golden. Serve warm or cold.

Sausage and Sage Paninis

Mix together 50 g (2 oz) butter, 1 tablespoon chopped sage leaves and 1 tablespoon wholegrain mustard, then spread over 4 pieces of white bread. Arrange 8 shop-bought cooked sausages, halved lengthways, over the sage butter. Top each with 2–3 slices of mozzarella cheese, then sandwich together with another slice of bread. Bake in a preheated oven, 220°C (425°F), Gas Mark 7, for 6–7 minutes until golden brown.

Cheese and Sage Straws

Unroll 375 g (12 oz) chilled ready-rolled puff pastry and lay on a clean surface with a short edge facing you. Spread the pastry thinly with 3–4 teaspoons Dijon mustard. Scatter 3 teaspoons chopped sage or 2 teaspoons dried sage over the bottom half of the pastry, then cover evenly with 25 g (1 oz) finely grated Parmesan cheese. Fold the top half of the pastry over the cheese and sandwich together.

Roll lightly with a rolling pin, then cut into about 20 x 1.5 cm (¾ inch) strips. Twist each strip and place, well spaced apart, on a baking sheet lined with nonstick baking paper. Bake in a preheated oven, 220°C (425°F), Gas Mark 7, for 10–12 minutes until crisp and golden. Transfer to wire racks to cool slightly, then serve warm with dips.

CAK-SAVO-BYJ

10 Tomato and Olive Filo Tartlets

Makes 12

6 sheets of filo pastry, about
30 x 40 cm (12 x 16 inches)
75 g (3 oz) unsalted butter,
melted
175 g (6 oz) baby plum tomatoes,
quartered
75 g (3 oz) mini mozzarella balls,
quartered
50 g (2 oz) pitted Kalamata olives
in oil, drained and roughly
chopped
2 spring onions, finely sliced
12 basil leaves, shredded
1 tablespoon extra virgin olive oil
salt and pepper
balsamic glaze, to serve

- Lay the filo sheets on a clean surface and brush each with melted butter, then place in 2 stacks of 3 sheets. Cut each stack into 6 rectangles, each 15 x 13 cm (6 x 5½ inches), then use to line a 12-hole shallow bun tray. Bake in a preheated oven, 220°C (425°F), Gas Mark 7, for 7–8 minutes until crisp and golden.

- Meanwhile, place the tomatoes, mozzarella, olives, spring onions and basil in a bowl. Drizzle over the oil, then season well and mix to combine.

- Transfer the pastry cases to a wire rack and spoon in the tomato and olive filling. Serve drizzled with balsamic glaze.

 20 Tomato and Olive Tarts

Unroll 375 g (12 oz) chilled ready-rolled puff pastry and cut into 4 rectangles. Place on a greased baking sheet and score a 1 cm (½ inch) border around the pastry edges. Bake in a preheated oven, 220°C (425°F), Gas Mark 7, for 7–8 minutes until lightly golden. Spread the centres with 1 teaspoon olive tapenade. Scatter over 250 g (8 oz) halved cherry tomatoes, 50 g (2 oz) pitted black olives and 2 thinly sliced spring onions, then drizzle with olive oil, season and bake for a further 6–7 minutes. Serve hot, with a green salad.

 30 Tomato and Olive Tarte Tatin

Heat 2 tablespoons olive oil in a 30 cm (12 inch) ovenproof frying pan, add 7–8 halved and seasoned plum tomatoes (enough to fit snugly in the pan), cut side down, and fry over a medium-high heat for 7–8 minutes until golden, adding 2 chopped garlic cloves 1 minute before the end of the cooking time. Meanwhile, roll out 250 g (8 oz) chilled puff or shortcrust pastry on a floured surface and cut out a round about 1 cm (½ inch) larger than the pan. Add 50 g (2 oz) drained and pitted Kalamata olives in oil to the pan, pushing them down so that they fill any gaps. Lay the pastry over the pan, carefully tucking it in around the edges to completely cover the filling. Place in a preheated oven, 220°C (425°F), Gas Mark 7, for 18–20 minutes until the pastry is puffed and golden. Invert on to a serving plate, drizzle with 1 tablespoon each olive oil and shop-bought balsamic glaze and scatter over 12 shredded basil leaves. Cut into 4–6 wedges and serve with peppery rocket leaves, if liked.

Spelt and Onion Seed Scones

Makes 7–8

200 g (7 oz) spelt flour, plus extra for dusting
½ teaspoon salt
2½ teaspoons baking powder
½ teaspoon powdered mustard
50 g (2 oz) unsalted butter, softened
1½ teaspoons black onion seeds, plus extra for sprinkling
1 large egg, lightly beaten
2–3 tablespoons natural yogurt

- Line 1 large baking sheet with nonstick baking paper. Sift the flour, salt, baking powder and mustard into a large bowl. Add the butter and rub in with the fingertips until the mixture resembles fine breadcrumbs. Stir in the onion seeds.

- Whisk together the egg and yogurt in a jug, reserving 1 tablespoon to glaze. Pour into the dry ingredients and mix to form a soft dough.

- Turn the dough out on to a floured surface and roll out to 1.5 cm (¾ inch) thick, then stamp out 7 or 8 rounds using a 6 cm (2½ inch) plain cutter, without twisting the cutter. Place on the prepared baking sheet and brush with the reserved glaze, then sprinkle with onion seeds.

- Bake in a preheated oven, 220°C (425°F), Gas Mark 7, for 10–12 minutes until risen and golden. Serve warm.

 Mustard and Onion Seed Melts

Cut open 4 ciabatta rolls. Lightly beat 2 large eggs in a bowl and add 2 tablespoons wholegrain mustard, 150 g (5 oz) mature grated Cheddar cheese and 2 teaspoons onion seeds. Season with salt and pepper, then spread evenly over the cut sides. Place on a baking sheet lined with nonstick baking paper and bake in a preheated oven, 220°C (425°F), Gas Mark 7, for 6–8 minutes until bubbling and golden. Serve with coleslaw and crudités.

 Spelt and Red Onion Scones

Heat 1 tablespoon olive oil in a frying pan, add 1 finely chopped red onion and cook for 7–8 minutes until softened and lightly golden. Meanwhile, prepare the scone dough as above, adding the cooked onion with the egg and yogurt. Tip the dough on to a baking sheet lined with nonstick baking paper and shape into a rectangle, about 20 x 12 cm (8 x 5 inches) and 1.5 cm (¾ inch) thick. Cut down through the dough to make 8 pieces, without separating the scones. Brush with the reserved glaze and sprinkle over the onion seeds or a little thinly sliced red onion. Bake in a preheated oven, 220°C (425°F), Gas Mark 7, for 12–15 minutes until risen and golden. Serve warm.

 # Smoked Salmon and Chive Pinwheels

Makes 22–26

4 slices of wholemeal bread,
   crusts removed
3 tablespoons cream cheese
2 teaspoons chopped chives
150 g (5 oz) thinly sliced smoked
   salmon
2 teaspoons lemon juice
freshly ground black pepper
lemon wedges, to serve

- Place the bread on a clean board and flatten with a rolling pin. Spread the cream cheese evenly over the bread slices, then scatter with the chives and top with the salmon. Squeeze over a little lemon juice and season with black pepper.

- Roll up the bread tightly, then use a sharp knife to cut into 22–26 x 1 cm (½ inch) slices. Place on a large serving dish, sprinkle with extra black pepper and serve with lemon wedges.

 Smoked Salmon and Chive Tartlets

Unroll 325 g (11 oz) chilled ready-rolled shortcrust pastry and cut out 4 x 12 cm (5 inch) rounds, then use to line 4 greased tartlet tins, trimming away any excess pastry. Place on a baking sheet. Cut 125 g (4 oz) thinly sliced smoked salmon into strips and divide between the tartlets with 25 g (1 oz) roughly chopped watercress leaves. Lightly beat 2 large eggs, 75 g (3 oz) cream cheese with chives and 3 tablespoons milk in a jug. Season well with crushed pink or black peppercorns and divide the mixture between the tartlets. Bake in a preheated oven, 220°C (425°F), Gas Mark 7, for 15 minutes, or until risen and golden. Serve warm or cold with a watercress and rocket salad and lemon wedges.

 Smoked Salmon and Chive Parcels

Beat together 75 ml (3 fl oz) single cream, 175 g (6 oz) cream cheese, 2 tablespoons chopped chives and ¼ teaspoon crushed pink peppercorns in a large bowl. Add 50 g (2 oz) roughly chopped watercress leaves, and 350 g (11½ oz) lightly smoked salmon fillet, cut into 1 cm (½ inch) slices, and mix gently to combine. Brush 4 sheets of filo pastry, about 45 x 25 cm (18 x 10 inches), with melted unsalted butter, then fold in half widthways. Spoon the salmon mixture on to the pastry, then roll up like parcels, tucking in the sides. Place on a baking sheet lined with nonstick baking paper and bake in a preheated oven, 200°C (400°F), Gas Mark 6, for 15 minutes, or until the pastry is golden and the fish is just cooked through. Serve with a rocket and watercress salad and a drizzle of warmed hollandaise sauce, if liked.

CAK-SAVO-JYQ

30 Chicken, Stilton and Potato Pies

Serves 4

2 potatoes, about 450 g (14½ oz)
in total
25 g (1 oz) unsalted butter, plus
extra 1 tablespoon, melted
1 tablespoon olive oil
175 g (6 oz) leek, trimmed
and sliced
150 g (5 oz) ready-made cheese,
carbonara or béchamel sauce
225 g (7½ oz) shop-bought
roasted chicken breast fillets,
shredded
75 g (3 oz) mature Stilton cheese,
crumbled
1 tablespoon chopped chives
3 thinly sliced spring onions
green salad, to serve

- Cook the potatoes in a saucepan of lightly salted boiling water for 8 minutes until just tender.

- Meanwhile, heat the butter and oil in a frying pan. Add the leek and cook, stirring occasionally, for 7–8 minutes until softened. Tip into a bowl, then add the cheese sauce, shredded chicken and crumbled Stilton and mix until combined.

- Drain the potatoes and, wearing rubber gloves to protect your hands from the heat, coarsely grate them into a bowl. Add the chives, spring onions and the 1 tablespoon melted butter and toss together.

- Spoon the leek and chicken mixture into 4 x 200 ml (7 fl oz) individual pie dishes, then heap the potato mixture on top. Bake in a preheated oven, 220°C (425°F), Gas Mark 7, for 15–18 minutes until crisp and golden.

- Serve with a crisp green salad, if liked.

Potato and Stilton Farls

Place 400 g (13 oz) shop-bought or leftover mashed potato, 75 g (3 oz) plain flour and 50 g (2 oz) crumbled mature Stilton in a large bowl. Season with salt and pepper and mix to form a soft dough. Turn out on to a floured surface and knead gently until smooth. Form into a 23 cm (9 inch) round and use a sharp knife to cut into 4 or 8 triangles. Cook in a dry, nonstick frying pan over a medium heat for about 4 minutes on each side until golden.

Free-Form Potato and Stilton Scones

Sift 200 g (7 oz) self-raising flour, 1 teaspoon salt and 2 teaspoons baking powder into a large bowl. Add 50 g (2 oz) softened unsalted butter and rub in with the fingertips until the mixture resembles fine breadcrumbs. Add 125 g (4 oz) shop-bought or leftover mashed potato and rub into the flour. Stir in 75 g (3 oz) crumbled Stilton, 2 finely sliced spring onions, 1 tablespoon chopped chives and a generous pinch of cracked black pepper. Add 100 ml (3½ fl oz) cold milk and mix to form a soft dough. Take handfuls of the dough and place in 12 slightly flattened, rough mounds on 2 baking sheets lined with nonstick baking paper. Bake in a preheated oven, 220°C (425°F), Gas Mark 7, for 10–12 minutes until golden. Serve split in half with cottage cheese or cream cheese.

 Cheese and Chive Crisps

Makes 12–15

75 g (3 oz) Parmesan cheese,
  finely grated
2 tablespoons finely chopped
  chives or 2 teaspoons dried
  chives
freshly ground black pepper

- Line a large baking sheet with nonstick baking paper. Mix together the cheese, chives and a generous pinch of black pepper in a bowl.

- Place a 9 cm (3¾ inch) plain cutter on the prepared baking sheet and evenly sprinkle 1 rounded tablespoon of the mixture inside. Remove the cutter and repeat with the remaining mixture to make 12–15 crisps.

- Bake in a preheated oven, 200°C (400°F), Gas Mark 6, for 5–7 minutes until golden. Carefully transfer to a wire rack to cool and crisp.

 Cheese and Chive Sablés

Sift 125 g (4 oz) plain flour, 1 teaspoon paprika and a pinch of salt and pepper into a bowl. Stir in 2 tablespoons finely chopped chives and 50 g (2 oz) finely grated Parmesan cheese. Add 50 g (2 oz) melted unsalted butter and enough of 1–2 tablespoons milk to form a soft dough. Knead lightly on a floured surface. Roll out to 2–3 mm (⅛ inch) thick, then stamp out about 24 rounds using a 5 cm (2 inch) fluted cutter. Place on 2 baking sheets lined with nonstick baking paper and bake in a preheated oven, 200°C (400°F), Gas Mark 6, for 8–10 minutes until golden. Transfer to wire racks to cool.

 Cheese and Chive Crackers

Beat together 75 g (3 oz) softened unsalted butter, 75 g (3 oz) finely grated Parmesan cheese, 2 tablespoons finely chopped chives and a pinch of salt and pepper in a bowl. Add 125 g (4 oz) plain flour and mix to form a soft dough, adding 1–2 teaspoons milk if necessary. Wrap in clingfilm and chill for 10–15 minutes. Roll out the dough on a floured surface to 2–3 mm (⅛ inch) thick, then stamp out about 24 rounds using a 5 cm (2 inch) cutter. Place on 2 baking sheets, lined with nonstick baking paper, and bake in a preheated oven, 200°C (400°F), Gas Mark 6, for 10 minutes, or until lightly golden. Transfer to wire racks to cool.

Chilli Cheese Explosion Scones

Makes 12–14

200 g (7 oz) self-raising flour
1 teaspoon salt
1 teaspoon baking powder
1 teaspoon paprika (optional)
¼ teaspoon cayenne pepper
1 red chilli, deseeded if liked and
  finely chopped
100 g (3½ oz) double Gloucester
  cheese, coarsely grated
1 tablespoon chopped chives
¼ teaspoon freshly ground
  black pepper
1 large egg, lightly beaten
3 tablespoons olive oil
2–3 tablespoons milk, plus extra
  to glaze
cream cheese, to serve

- Line a large baking sheet with nonstick baking paper. Sift the flour, salt, baking powder, paprika, if using, and cayenne into a bowl. Stir in the chilli, 75 g (3 oz) of the cheese and the chives, then add the black pepper. Pour in the egg and oil and enough of the milk to form a soft dough.

- Turn the dough out on to a floured surface and roll out to 1.5 cm (¾ inch) thick, then stamp out 12–14 rounds using a 5 cm (2 inch) plain or fluted cutter. Place on the prepared baking sheet, brush with extra milk and sprinkle over the remaining cheese.

- Bake in a preheated oven, 220°C (425°F), Gas Mark 7, for 10 minutes, or until golden brown. Transfer to wire racks to cool slightly, then split the scones open and serve warm with cream cheese.

 Chilli Cheese Soda Farls

Mix together 100 g (3½ oz) grated mature double Gloucester cheese, 1 finely chopped red chilli, 1 tablespoon chopped parsley, 1 teaspoon paprika and ¼ teaspoon each of cayenne and black pepper. Split 4 soda farls in half and spread with 100 g (3½ oz) cream cheese. Place in an ovenproof dish and sprinkle over the cheese mixture. Bake in a preheated oven, 230°C (450°F), Gas Mark 8, for 7–8 minutes until crispy. Scatter with pickled jalapeño pepper slices and serve with soured cream.

 Chilli Cheese Explosion Muffins

Sift 225 g (7½ oz) plain flour, 1 teaspoon paprika, ¼ teaspoon cayenne pepper, 1½ teaspoons baking powder and ½ teaspoon salt into a large bowl. Add 50 g (2 oz) softened unsalted butter and rub in with the fingertips until the mixture resembles fine breadcrumbs, then stir in 1 red chilli, deseeded if liked and finely chopped, 75 g (3 oz) grated mature double Gloucester cheese, ¼ teaspoon black pepper and 1 tablespoon chopped parsley or chives. Whisk together 1 large egg, 125 ml (4 fl oz) milk and 75 ml (3 fl oz) vegetable oil in a jug. Pour into the dry ingredients and stir until just combined. Spoon the mixture into 10–12 holes of a well-greased 12-hole nonstick muffin tin and sprinkle with an extra 25 g (1 oz) grated double Gloucester. Bake in a preheated oven, 200°C 400°F), Gas Mark 6, for 18–20 minutes until risen and golden.

CAK-SAVO-NUC

Chicken and Taleggio Deep-Filled Pies

Serves 4

375 g (12 oz) chilled ready-rolled wholemeal or plain shortcrust pastry

butter, for greasing

200 g (7 oz) shop-bought roasted chicken breast fillets, thickly sliced

150 g (5 oz) Taleggio cheese, sliced

8 shop-bought slow-roasted or sun-dried tomatoes, roughly chopped

beaten egg, to glaze

steamed vegetables or mixed salad leaves, to serve (optional)

- Unroll the pastry and cut into 4 x 12 cm (5 inch) rounds, then use to line 4 greased giant muffin or deep Yorkshire pudding tins, each about 10 cm (4 inches) in diameter and 4.5 cm (2 inches) deep. Trim the excess pastry, leaving 1 cm (½ inch) above the tins, and place the tins on a baking sheet. Reroll the pastry trimmings and stamp out 4 x 10 cm (4 inch) rounds and set aside.

- Pile up the chicken, Taleggio and tomatoes in the centre of each pie. Top with the pastry lids and crimp together the edges of the pastry to seal. Brush with a little beaten egg and cut out a small slit or circle from the top of each one.

- Bake in a preheated oven, 220°C (425°F), Gas Mark 7, for 12–14 minutes until golden brown. Serve hot with steamed vegetables or a mixed leaf salad, if liked.

 Cheesy Chicken Flatbreads

Place 2 large flatbreads or ready-made pizza bases on baking sheets and spread 1 tablespoon sun-dried tomato paste evenly over the surface of each. Scatter with 200 g (7 oz) shop-bought roasted chicken breast fillets, sliced, and top with 175 g (6 oz) sliced Taleggio cheese. Sprinkle with 1 teaspoon dried thyme and bake in a preheated oven, 230°C (450°F), Gas Mark 8, for 7–8 minutes until bubbling and golden. Cut each flatbread in half and serve with salad.

 Chicken and Cheese Mini Loaves Sift 225 g (7½ oz) plain flour, 1½ teaspoons baking powder and ½ teaspoon salt into a bowl. Add 50 g (2 oz) softened unsalted butter and rub in with the fingertips until the mixture resembles fine breadcrumbs, then stir in 1 teaspoon dried thyme, 75 g (3 oz) diced Taleggio cheese and 75 g (3 oz) shop-bought roasted chicken breast fillets, finely diced. Whisk together 1 large egg, 125 ml (4 fl oz) milk and 75 ml (3 fl oz) vegetable oil in a jug. Pour into the dry ingredients and stir until just combined. Spoon the mixture into 10–12 holes of a well-greased 12-hole mini loaf tin, top with an extra slice of Taleggio and bake in a preheated oven, 200°C (400°F), Gas Mark 6, for 18–20 minutes until risen and golden.

CAK-SAVO-HIP

1️⃣0️⃣ Spicy Dippers

Makes 32

1 tablespoon olive or vegetable oil
4 corn tortillas
2 teaspoons Mexican or preferred
   spice mix
salsas and dips, to serve

- Brush the oil lightly over the corn tortillas. Sprinkle ½ teaspoon of the spice mix evenly over each tortilla, then cut each tortilla into 8 wedges.

- Place the wedges, spice side up, on 2 large baking sheets and bake in a preheated oven, 200°C (400°F), Gas Mark 6, for 5–7 minutes until crisp. Transfer to wire racks to cool slightly, then serve warm with salsas and dips.

2️⃣ Cheese Dippers

Cut 1 small ciabatta loaf into about 25 x 5–10 mm (¼–½ inch) slices. Brush each slice with a little olive oil or melted butter and place the slices on 2 baking sheets. Mix together ½ teaspoon garlic powder, 1 teaspoon onion powder, 1 teaspoon dried oregano and ½ teaspoon paprika in a small bowl. Toss with 50 g (2 oz) finely grated Parmesan or mature Cheddar cheese and sprinkle over the ciabatta slices. Place in a preheated oven, 200°C (400°F), Gas Mark 6, for 8–10 minutes until crisp and golden. Transfer to wire racks to cool slightly, then serve the crostinis warm with dips.

3️⃣ Herby Dippers

Beat together 50 g (2 oz) softened unsalted butter, 50 g (2 oz) cream cheese with chives, 25 g (1 oz) finely grated Parmesan cheese and a pinch of salt and pepper in a bowl. Add 150 g (5 oz) plain flour and stir until combined, adding 1–2 teaspoons milk, if necessary, to form a smooth dough. Wrap in clingfilm and chill for 10 minutes. Roll out the dough on a floured surface to 2–3 mm (⅛ inch) thick, then stamp out 20–22 rounds using a 6 cm (2½ inch) plain cutter. Place on 2 baking sheets lined with nonstick baking paper and brush the tops with a little milk. Sprinkle each dipper with a pinch of chopped chives and bake in a preheated oven, 200°C (400°F), Gas Mark 6, for 10 minutes, or until lightly golden. Transfer to wire racks to cool slightly, then serve the dippers warm with dips.

30 Caramelized Onion and Cheddar Pasties

Serves 4

500 g (1 lb) chilled puff pastry
flour, for dusting
4 tablespoons caramelized onion
  chutney
200 g (7 oz) shop-bought or
  leftover mashed potato, or
  roughly diced cooked potatoes
150 g (5 oz) mature Cheddar
  cheese, coarsely grated
2 teaspoons chopped thyme
  leaves or 4 teaspoons chopped
  chives
beaten egg, to glaze
salt and pepper

• Line a large baking sheet with nonstick baking paper. Roll out the pastry on a floured surface and cut out 4 x 20 cm (8 inch) rounds, rerolling the trimmings if necessary. Spread 1 tablespoon of the chutney over the centre of each circle, leaving a 1.5 cm (¾ inch) border around the edge.

• Spoon the potato into the middle of each one and sprinkle over the cheese and thyme or chives. Season with salt and pepper. Brush the border with a little beaten egg and fold the pastry over, encasing the filling. Press the edges together to seal.

• Place the pasties on the prepared baking sheet, brush with beaten egg and cut 2 small slits in the top of each. Bake in a preheated oven, 220°C (425°F), Gas Mark 7, for about 15–18 minutes until puffed and golden.

---

1 Cheesy Caramelized Onion Crostinis Slice 1 small baguette into 16–20 slices, then place on a baking sheet. Drizzle with olive oil, sprinkle with sea salt flakes and bake in a preheated oven, 220°C (425°F), Gas Mark 7, for 3–5 minutes until golden and toasted. Spoon ½ teaspoon caramelized onion chutney on to each, then top each with a thin slice of mature Cheddar cheese and sprinkle with a pinch of chopped thyme leaves. Serve the crostinis warm.

2 Cheese and Onion Vol au Vents Place 16 mini vol au vent cases on a baking sheet and bake in a preheated oven, 230°C (450°F), Gas Mark 8, for 10 minutes, or according to the packet instructions, until puffed and lightly golden. Spoon 1 teaspoon caramelized onion chutney into each, then scatter 100 g (3½ oz) grated mature Cheddar cheese and a scant sprinkling of fresh or dried thyme over the vol au vents. Return to the oven for 1–2 minutes, or until the cheese is just melting. Serve warm.

CAK-SAVO-PYG

30 Sweet Chilli Mini Cornbreads

Makes 12

175 g (6 oz) fine cornmeal
100 g (3½ oz) plain flour
1½ teaspoons baking powder
1 teaspoon salt
25 g (1 oz) caster sugar
1 large egg
3 tablespoons sweet chilli jam or
  sauce
200 ml (7 fl oz) milk
100 ml (3½ fl oz) vegetable oil,
  plus extra for greasing

- Mix together the cornmeal, flour, baking powder, salt and sugar in a bowl.

- Whisk together the egg, sweet chilli jam, milk and vegetable oil in a jug. Pour into the dry ingredients and stir until just combined and the batter is smooth. Leave to stand for 5 minutes.

- Spoon the batter into a well-greased 12-hole nonstick muffin or mini loaf tin and bake in a preheated oven, 220°C (425°F), Gas Mark 7, for 15 minutes, or until risen and golden. Transfer to a wire rack to cool slightly, then serve warm.

---

10 Sweet Chilli Toasts Cut 1 baguette diagonally into 8 long slices and spread each one with 1 teaspoon sweet chilli jam. Scatter over a drained 200 g (7 oz) can sweetcorn and sprinkle over 150 g (5 oz) grated Emmental or Cheddar cheese. Place on a baking sheet and bake in a preheated oven, 220°C (425°F), Gas Mark 7, for 6–7 minutes until bubbling and golden.

20 Sweet Chilli Cornbread Griddles Mix together 100 g (3½ oz) fine cornmeal, 75 g (3 oz) plain flour, 2 teaspoons bicarbonate of soda and 1 teaspoon salt in a bowl. Whisk together 1 large egg, 200 ml (7 fl oz) buttermilk, 2 tablespoons sweet chilli jam or sauce and 2 tablespoons vegetable oil in a jug, then pour into the dry ingredients and mix until the batter is smooth and thick. Heat 1 tablespoon vegetable oil in a smooth griddle pan or heavy-based, nonstick frying pan, add spoonfuls of the batter and cook over a low heat for 1–2 minutes until bubbles start to appear on the surface, then flip over and cook for a further 1–2 minutes until risen and golden. Repeat with the remaining batter to make 14–18 griddles, adding more oil to the pan if necessary. Serve warm with extra sweet chilli jam or sauce for dipping.

20 Blue Cheese and Parma Ham Cigars

Makes 12

6 sheets of filo pastry, about
30 x 40 cm (12 x 16 inches)

75 g (3 oz) unsalted butter,
melted

12 very thin slices of Parma ham

175 g (6 oz) strong blue cheese,
crumbled

75 g (3 oz) walnut pieces,
chopped

3 spring onions, finely sliced

creamy herb dip, to serve
(optional)

• Line 2 baking sheets with nonstick baking paper. Lay the stack of filo sheets on a clean surface, then cut in half widthways and keep covered with clingfilm.

• Brush 1 filo sheet with melted butter, then cover with a slice of Parma ham and scatter over a little of the blue cheese, crushed walnuts and spring onions. Starting at a short end, roll up like a cigar, tucking in the sides when you have rolled about two-thirds of the pastry. Continue rolling, then place on the prepared baking sheet. Repeat with the remaining ingredients to make 12 rolls.

• Brush the cigars with the remaining melted butter and bake in a preheated oven, 220°C (425°F), Gas Mark 7, for 8–10 minutes until crisp and golden. Serve warm with a creamy herb dip, if liked.

 Blue Cheese and Parma Ham Focaccia Spread 4 tablespoons red onion chutney over 1 large focaccia loaf. Lay 12 slices of Parma ham over the top in folds, then crumble over 175 g (6 oz) strong blue cheese. Drizzle with 2 teaspoons olive oil and place on a baking sheet. Bake in a preheated oven, 220°C (425°F), Gas Mark 7, for 6–7 minutes until hot and golden. Scatter with 75 g (3 oz) chopped walnut pieces and serve with a rocket and fig salad.

 Blue Cheese and Parma Ham Tart Roll out 375 g (12 oz) chilled puff pastry on a floured surface to 30 x 40 cm (12 x 16 inches) and place on a large baking sheet lined with nonstick baking paper. Brush with melted unsalted butter and score a 1.5 cm (¾ inch) border around the edge. Cut 6 ripe figs into quarters lengthways. Arrange 12 thin slices of Parma ham in folds over the pastry with the figs and scatter over 175 g (6 oz) crumbled strong blue cheese and 75 g (3 oz) chopped walnut pieces leaving the border clear. Bake in a preheated oven, 220°C (425°F), Gas Mark 7, for 20 minutes, or until crisp and golden. Serve warm with red onion chutney and green salad.

 # Easy Ginger-Baked Prawns

Serves 4

32 raw peeled king prawns

3 teaspoons pickled chopped ginger

2 tablespoons chopped coriander leaves, plus extra to garnish

1 red chilli, deseeded and chopped

1 teaspoon finely grated lime rind

1 tablespoon vegetable oil

2 teaspoons light soy sauce

- First, butterfly the prawns. Cut a deep slit down the back of each prawn, pushing it apart without slicing all the way through, then place in a bowl with the remaining ingredients and mix well to coat.

- Thread the prawns on to 4 metal skewers, then place across a roasting tin and bake in a preheated oven, 220°C (425°F), Gas Mark 7, for 6–7 minutes until hot and cooked through. Serve scattered with extra coriander.

 ### Prawn and Crab Tarts

Unroll a 325 g (11 oz) chilled ready-rolled shortcrust pastry and cut out 4 x 12 cm (5 inch) rounds, then use to line 4 greased fluted tartlet or quiche tins, trimming away any excess pastry. Place on a baking sheet. Mix together a drained 175 g (6 oz) can crab meat, 125 g (4 oz) cooked peeled prawns, thawed if frozen, 2 chopped spring onions and 2 tablespoons chopped coriander leaves in a bowl. Add 2 large lightly beaten eggs and 50 ml (2 fl oz) single cream and mix together. Spoon into the cases and bake in a preheated oven, 220°C (425°F), Gas Mark 7, for about 15 minutes until risen and golden. Serve with a crunchy Asian-style salad, if liked.

 ### Baked Prawn Spring Rolls

Heat 1 tablespoon vegetable oil in a wok or frying pan until hot, add 200 g (7 oz) roughly chopped, raw peeled prawns, 3 teaspoons pickled chopped ginger and 1 deseeded and chopped red chilli and stir-fry over a medium heat for about 2 minutes until the prawns turn pink and are cooked through. Scrape into a large bowl and toss with 2 tablespoons chopped coriander leaves, 1 teaspoon finely grated lime rind, 100 g (3½ oz) ready-cooked rice noodles and 2 tablespoons sweet chilli dipping sauce. Cut 4 sheets of filo pastry, about 30 x 40 cm (12 x 16 inches), in half widthways, then brush each with melted unsalted butter and sandwich together to make 4 pairs. Divide the prawn mixture between the pastry rectangles, then roll up from the short end, tucking in the sides. Place on a baking sheet lined with nonstick baking paper and bake in a preheated oven, 220°C (425°F), Gas Mark 7, for 12–15 minutes, until crisp and golden. Serve hot with extra dipping sauce.

20 Mozzarella and Pesto Mini Melt Muffins

Makes 18

150 g (5 oz) plain flour
1 teaspoon baking powder
¼ teaspoon salt
1 spring onion, finely sliced
¼ teaspoon freshly ground
  black pepper
1 large egg, lightly beaten
75 ml (3 fl oz) milk
50 ml (2 fl oz) vegetable oil
2 tablespoons good-quality
  ready-made pesto
50 g (2 oz) mozzarella cheese,
  cut into cubes
1 tablespoon pine nuts

- Line 18 holes of 2 x 12-hole nonstick mini muffin tins with paper mini muffin cases or lightly grease. Sift the flour, baking powder and salt into a large bowl, then stir in the spring onion and pepper.

- Whisk together the egg, milk, oil and pesto in a jug. Pour into the dry ingredients and stir until just combined.

- Spoon the mixture into the prepared mini muffin tins, then push a piece of cheese into the centre of each one and scatter over the pine nuts.

- Bake in a preheated oven, 200°C (400°F), Gas Mark 6, for 12–15 minutes until risen and golden. Serve warm.

 English Muffin Mozzarella Melts

Split 4 wholemeal English muffins in half and cook under a preheated hot grill for 1–2 minutes until golden and toasted. Spread each cut side with 1 teaspoon good-quality ready-made pesto. Divide 16 halved cherry tomatoes between the muffins and scatter over 1 finely sliced spring onion. Lay 125 g (4 oz) sliced mozzarella cheese over the tomatoes and return to the grill for 3–4 minutes until melted. Serve scattered with toasted pine nuts and basil leaves.

 Melting Cheese and Pesto Muffins

Sift 200 g (7 oz) plain flour, 1 teaspoon baking powder, ¾ teaspoon bicarbonate of soda and ½ teaspoon salt into a large bowl, then stir in 3 tablespoons grated Parmesan cheese and ¼ teaspoon freshly ground black pepper. Whisk together 250 g (8 oz) natural yogurt, 50 ml (2 fl oz) milk, 3 tablespoons groundnut oil, 2 large lightly beaten eggs, 2 tablespoons good-quality ready-made pesto, 50 g (2 oz) diced mozzarella cheese and 50 g (2 oz) chopped sun-dried tomatoes in a jug or large bowl. Pour into the dry ingredients and stir until just combined. Spoon the mixture into a greased or muffin case-lined 12-hole nonstick muffin tin, then scatter over 1 tablespoon pine nuts and 50 g (2 oz) diced mozzarella. Bake in a preheated oven, 200°C (400°F), Gas Mark 6, for 18–20 minutes until risen, golden and firm to the touch. Serve warm.

CAK-SAVO-HYE

2 ⏱ Bacon and Brie Strudels

Serves 4

6 sheets of filo pastry, about
   30 x 40 cm (12 x 16 inches)
100 g (3½ oz) unsalted butter,
   melted
150 g (5 oz) firm brie, thinly sliced
75 g (3 oz) shop-bought cooked
   smoked bacon, roughly chopped
150 g (5 oz) cherry tomatoes,
   quartered
3 tablespoons toasted pine nuts

To serve

chutney
Little Gem lettuce

- Line a baking sheet with nonstick baking paper. Lay the filo sheets on a clean surface, then cut in half widthways and brush each sheet with melted butter. Place in 4 stacks of 3 sheets with the long edges facing you.

- Divide the brie, bacon, cherry tomatoes and pine nuts between the stacks, placing on the bottom half of each, then roll up the strudels away from you, tucking in the sides when you have rolled two-thirds of the pastry.

- Place the strudels on the prepared baking sheet, brush with the remaining butter and bake in a preheated oven, 230°C (450°F), Gas Mark 8, for 10–12 minutes until crisp and golden. Serve hot with chutney and Little Gem lettuce.

 Brie and Bacon Croutons

Cut 1 small, granary baguette into about 16 x 1.5 cm (¾ inch) slices. Crumble over 75 g (3 oz) shop-bought cooked bacon, then divide 150 g (5 oz) sliced firm brie between the slices. Place on a large baking sheet lined with nonstick baking paper and bake in a preheated oven, 200°C (400°F), Gas Mark 6, for 6–7 minutes until the bread is crisp and the brie is melted and golden. Place mixed baby leaves on 4 serving plates and top with the croutons. Serve warm.

 Bacon and Brie Tart

Roll out 375 g (12 oz) chilled puff pastry on a floured surface to 30 x 40 cm (12 x 16 inches) and place on a large baking sheet lined with nonstick baking paper. Brush with melted unsalted butter and score a 1.5 cm (¾ inch) border around the edge. Bake in a preheated oven, 220°C (425°F), Gas Mark 7, for 8–10 minutes until pale golden. Meanwhile, heat 2 tablespoons olive oil in a nonstick frying pan, add 1 large sliced red onion and cook for 7–8 minutes until

softened and golden. Remove the pastry from the oven and scatter over the red onion, leaving the border clear. Top with 75 g (3 oz) roughly torn shop-bought cooked bacon, 150 g (5 oz) halved cherry tomatoes and 150 g (5 oz) thinly sliced, firm brie. Sprinkle over 2 teaspoons thyme leaves and return to the oven for a further 7–8 minutes until crisp and golden. Scatter with toasted pine nuts and serve warm with Little Gem salad leaves.

1 Grilled Pepper, Spinach and Cheese Muffins

Serves 4

4 shop-bought wholemeal
  English muffins
50 g (2 oz) unsalted butter,
  softened
75 g (3 oz) baby spinach leaves,
  plus extra to serve
200 g (7 oz) roasted peppers in
  oil, drained and sliced
1 small red onion, thinly sliced
150 g (5 oz) blue cheese, such as
  Stilton, Roquefort or Saint Agur
apple chutney, to serve

- Slice each muffin in half horizontally and spread the cut sides with the butter.

- Heat a large, nonstick frying pan over a medium-high heat, add the muffins, cut sides down, and cook for about 1–2 minutes until crisp and golden. Arrange cut side up on a baking sheet or in an ovenproof dish.

- Scatter over the spinach, roasted peppers, red onion and cheese and cook under a preheated grill for 2–3 minutes until melted. Serve warm with extra spinach leaves and apple chutney.

---

2 Pepper and Cheese Mini Muffins

Sift 150 g (5 oz) plain flour,
1 teaspoon baking powder,
½ teaspoon bicarbonate of soda
and ¼ teaspoon salt into a bowl,
then stir in 2 tablespoons grated
Parmesan cheese. Whisk together
1 large lightly beaten egg, 100 ml
(3½ fl oz) milk, 50 ml (2 fl oz)
vegetable oil and 1 tablespoon
chopped parsley in a jug, then stir
in 75 g (3 oz) mixed peppers in
oil, drained and chopped. Pour
into the dry ingredients and stir
until just combined. Spoon the
mixture into 18–24 holes of 2 case-
lined 12-hole mini muffin tins and
scatter with 2 tablespoons pine
nuts. Bake in a preheated oven,
200°C (400°F), Gas Mark 6, for
12–14 minutes until risen and
golden. Serve warm.

3 Spicy Pepper and Cheese Muffins

Sift 250 g (8 oz) plain flour,
2 teaspoons baking powder and
¼ teaspoon salt into a large
bowl, then stir in 15 g (½ oz)
Mexican spice mix and
¼ teaspoon freshly ground black
pepper. Whisk together 2 large
lightly beaten eggs, 150 ml
(¼ pint) milk and 150 ml (¼ pint)
vegetable oil in a jug. Pour into
the dry ingredients, add 2 sliced
spring onions, 100 g (3½ oz)
crumbled feta cheese,
2 tablespoons chopped parsley
and 150 g (5 oz) mixed peppers
in oil, drained and sliced, and
stir until just combined. Spoon
the mixture into a greased or
muffin case-lined 12-hole
nonstick muffin tin and bake in
a preheated oven, 180°C

(350°F) Gas Mark 4, for
20 minutes, or until risen and
golden. Serve warm.

CAK-SAVO-HIX

Index

Page references in *italics* indicate photographs

Acknowledgements

Recipes by **Jo McAuley**
Executive Editor **Eleanor Maxfield**
Editor **Alex Stetter**
Copy Editor **Jo Murray**
Art Direction **Tracy Killick for Tracy Killick Art Direction and Design**
Original Design Concept **www.gradedesign.com**
Designer **Geoff Fennell for Tracy Killick Art Direction and Design**
Photographer **Stephen Conroy**
Home Economist **Denise Smart**
Stylist **Liz Hippisley**
Production **Lucy Carter**